KT-478-291

This book is due for return on ~~or before the last date~~ shown below.

-1. NOV. 2001

15. NOV 2002

RECRUITMENT AND SELECTION

P R Plumbley

Fifth edition

Institute of Personnel Management

First published 1968
Reprinted twice 1969
Second edition 1974
Third edition 1976
Reprinted 1978, 1981
Fourth edition 1985
Fifth edition 1991

British Library Cataloguing in Publication Data
Plumbley, Philip, *1931*–
 Recruitment and selection. – 4th ed.
 I. Title II. Institute of Personnel Management
 658.311

 ISBN 0852924593

Phototypeset by Intype, London
Printed in Great Britain by Billing and Sons Ltd, Worcester

The views expressed in this book are the author's own, and may not
necessarily reflect those of the IPM.

Contents

Foreword

When this book was first published, it had a sub-title: 'In a full employment economy'. The last twenty years have seen major changes; over-full employment has been replaced by massive unemployment as whole industries have been reshaped. Some claim that a second industrial revolution has been – or is – taking place. As I write, the economy is once again going from boom to recession. Executive redundancy is rising; certain industries are already feeling the pinch. Economic forecasters are predicting yet more change as the UK economy aligns and adapts itself to the wider European market.

The importance of people has at last begun to be recognized. Success and failure are increasingly seen to be due not to external influences but a direct result of poor management or trade union indifference. The industries which have survived and grown have been led by managements which are imaginative and adaptive, which have well-selected and well-trained employees and which have instituted working practices which enable them to be fulfilled – and thus to strive and achieve.

The skills of recruitment, assessment and selection have never been in greater demand. Consultancies, many of them staffed by redundant personnel people, have grown up like mushrooms. There is no shortage of help available, though the level of skill is often deplorably low. Yet there are no magic, black arts in recruitment and selection. There is a vast fund of knowledge readily available and demonstrable which can be effectively taught and applied. Good, professional recruitment and selection skills can be adapted to any changes in the economy; they are infinitely flexible in their application and can be learned by personnel professional and line manager without undue difficulty.

This book is designed for anyone involved in recruitment and selection. The format allows quick scanning to absorb the essential points, with more detailed information for the serious student and specialist practitioner. The case studies provide light relief as we look at how the process often happens in the real world – and how it is viewed by the parties concerned. The Bibliography at the end, although not exhaustive, points the way for those who wish to read even more widely.

Finally, I should like to record my debt to two former colleagues, the late Ron Denerley and Dominic McDonnell, for their help and inspiration with the original text, and to numerous colleagues and students for their helpful suggestions and criticisms which I have endeavoured to incorporate in this major revision to the text.

PRP
1991

Perspective

The nature of recruitment

People make companies. So do all those involved in the recruitment process.

People are the life-blood of any enterprise, they are its vital asset. On them depends everything else. Capital and ideas or inventions are sterile without people to activate them. But people are a very variable commodity with an infinite range of skills, aptitudes and personalities. In some jobs, it is true, people can be interchangeable; but people are not robots, however highly trained. Levels of skill may be interchangeable, but the people are as different as chalk from cheese. Some are adaptable; some promotable to supervisory roles. Some have physical or mental limitations; some will readily move geographically, others will not. And so on. Recruitment and selection is not simply about filling jobs; it is about building a workforce that is suitable and adaptable to suit the enterprise's changing needs.

If done thoroughly, recruitment is a time-consuming and costly business. If done badly, the cost may be incalculable, in terms of lost opportunity, lost customers and spoiled work. The loss to individuals may be even greater, in stress, loss of income and perhaps unemployment – all through no fault of their own. The 'buck and the tab' rest with management, as the Americans say.

Recruitment is a two-way process; both partners have the right of choice. While the dole is uncomfortable, it does provide a safety net in the last resort. Gone are the days of 'take it or leave it'. Today's candidate is unwilling to take things on trust and wants to know about the company, its profitability, longer-term plans and scope for the individual employee. As more and more companies turn to 'local bargaining', the 'rate for the job' has become a 'tailor-made package' including wages/salary, bonus and pension payments at virtually all levels. A contract must be made and signed and cannot legally be altered without the express agreement of the individual. Grievance procedures must be spelled out and termination clauses explained.

In the current economy, jobs have to be sold and at times taken to the individual either by a geographical move of office or factory or by 'home-working'. Flexitime has become the norm in some industries. Most common forms of discrimination – sexism, ageism, racial prejudice, religious intolerance – have been banned by law or by social pressure backed by tribunal and penalties. Trade union protectionism – the closed shop, preferred candidates, unreasonable restrictions in training – is likewise illegal, and professional restrictive practices are under attack. Woe betide the employer who does not know current Contract of Employment law and the Protection of Employment Act. EEC directives are increasingly attempting to codify 'best practice' among community countries, so we may expect to find even more restrictions on employers and protection for employees during the next decade.

Good employment is founded upon trust, and trust goes both ways. A trusting workforce will co-operate, give that little bit extra, not quibble about minor changes and inconveniences. Then communication will flow in both directions and everyone have the commercial health of the enterprise at heart. But trust is fragile and easily ruptured. It starts at the recruitment stage. Sadly, sheer bad manners and contempt for the individual are not uncommon. Letters are not answered – merely acknowledged and obviously not read. Little account is taken of the difficulty candidates may have in coming for interview at very short notice. Application forms are often badly designed and ask irrelevant questions – or questions which should more properly be left until later. Candidates are kept waiting without adequate explanation, and interviews are not planned or properly prepared. Candidates are also guilty of bad manners, of not turning up on time, of lying – or distorting the truth – at interview and hoping to 'get away with it'. The contrast between the attitude of one employer and another can be quite marked. Trust breeds trust; good admin and preparation are not bureaucratic niceties but a vital part of management, laying the foundations for the kind of employee relations which show up in the bottom line.

The background

Personnel selection as we know it today is a phenomenon of the twentieth century. Of course, it is not really new. Gideon chose his army from among those 'who were not fearful'; he then set them a test (the water drinking test) and prepared them for battle (Judges, 7.2–18)! The need to select and direct large numbers of people arose during the two Great Wars. The 1930s saw major developments in the behavioural sciences, which were then applied extensively during the Second World War. The vast sifting followed by training and field results in both military and civilian occupations allowed for major innovation and refinement on a scale rarely possible. The subsequent discharge and retraining saw wartime selection skills overtly applied to the selection of apprentices/trainees and management with some considerable success. Scientific selection techniques became respectable, although it took many years to convince the sceptics. They form the theoretical basis of this book, modified by the pragmatism necessary to relate to the 'real world' of everyday recruitment and selection of employees at all 'levels' of occupation.

An outline of this book

The recruitment and selection process can conveniently be divided into four distinct phases:

1 Analysing the need and the marketplace
2 Assembling a list of suitable candidates
3 Assessing the candidates
4 Negotiating a contract.

Before attempting to advertise a vacancy it is vital to have a clear idea as to the fundamental purpose of the job, where it fits into the whole organization and how it interacts with other jobs. When considering the type of person who might fill the post the recruiter must take stock of the marketplace – what types of people are available or might reasonably and economically be attracted to put their names forward. The second stage is determining the optimum method of assembling a list of possible candidates: internal trawl; advertising; trade fairs; recruiting drives at schools or colleges; executive search etc. Much will depend on the current fashions people adopt when looking for a job and how easy or difficult it is going to be to locate and attract a field of suitably qualified and experienced people.

Having got a list, the selection part of the process begins. If the demands of the job have been quantified in such a way that candidates can be measured using a common yardstick, 'gut feel' can give way to objective, scientific selection. The 7 Point Plan is one such yardstick which has stood the test of time as it is infinitely variable yet forces the selector to concentrate on what can reasonably be assessed and measured and reduces the scope for bias, guesswork and other flights of fancy! There are many 'tools of the trade' available to help in this part of the process, though they tend in practice to be reduced to four: application forms; tests; interviews; and references (the most popular and least reliable being interviews). The final stage is negotiation of the terms of contract, final reference checking and absorption of the new recruit into the workforce with the minimum of disruption, especially during the early learning and settling in period. Close attention to this makes for a well-motivated new recruit and can act as a spur to others to increase output and raise efficiency.

1

Analysing the need and the marketplace

'Need the job be filled at all?' is the first question to raise. It is surprising how often the question is not asked, let alone answered convincingly. There appears to be a built-in reflex which even 'head-count' restrictions fail to inhibit; someone leaving must be replaced as soon as possible. The facts often indicate otherwise.

Every vacancy presents management with an opportunity to rethink the structure of the organization and the allocation of duties. More fundamentally, it is a rare opportunity to reconsider the objectives of the enterprise or service and ask how they might best be served. There is also a choice; to act quickly to plug a gap or to spend a little longer looking at other courses of action first: splitting/combining the duties; re-allotting them; using the post as a training slot or for an older worker etc. The choice is wide, but that is what management is all about.

The first thing is to analyse the apparent need in all its facets: the actual job as it is being done currently (or as proposed it should be done); its purpose in the overall organization structure and allocation of duties or tasks; how it interlocks with other jobs both within and outside the department; the resources available (equipment, capital and revenue, people etc); and methodology currently employed. This has then to be translated into human terms: the skills and experience needed to do the job effectively, training available for the newcomer. Psychological and domestic disturbance may follow; if so, the source of stress must be considered, and whether or not it reasonably 'goes with job' or has been created by the management culture. Most jobs are not currently being performed by robots; people mould and adapt them to suit their own individual strengths and weaknesses, likes and dislikes. Management has had a hand in this and so the job frequently reflects the style of the present – and possibly a succession of former – managers. Change the scope for the individual and the job changes. In spite of a series of recessions, take-overs,

11

mergers and massive reorganizations, commentators maintain that the comparatively low wage economy in the UK still conceals a good deal of hidden redundancy – perhaps as high as 10% in some industries. Much of this could be rooted out without too much individual distress by following the approach set out in this chapter. It is still fashionable to talk of 'round and square pegs to be fitted into round or square holes'; the analogy is becoming archaic, but the principle is thoroughly up-to-date. To accurately determine the shape of the hole is the first key step.

Job descriptions

So much for the philosophy! Now to get down to basics. Most managers (hopefully) keep records of their decisions, which will start with the *Title of the Job* followed by internal details for means of identification or classification. The *Purpose of the Job* should follow – a short, pithy statement which encapsulates the job and which can be referred to whenever in doubt. Practice varies, but many now write a few paragraphs describing the job. While 'boxes' and guidelines can help, the writer should not be artificially constrained as this can lead to important aspects being overlooked.

Next comes a *detailed description* which attempts to quantify and break the job down into specific parts or tasks or responsibilities. If this sounds tedious or irrelevant to someone in a small organization it is the thought process that counts, however simply it is recorded. Moreover, this kind of document will need to be referred to in the future – especially if a dispute arises – and will be invaluable whenever jobs are reviewed as the organization grows or contracts.

While a job description can be written in the office, a visit to the site is very worthwhile if not imperative. All one's antennae should be operational; look at the location, the working conditions, the state and type of equipment used, the management culture (every department is different in some aspects) and the other people there with whom the newcomer must integrate. If the job is a mobile one, try to visit at least one significant site: a customer the salesperson will have to sell to; a typical construction site for that industry; a factory workshop and so on. Watch how jobs are being performed. With the manager's and operative's permission talk to someone doing the job or a similar one and note how the job is approached, the demands of feeder or user departments met. Find out what the present incumbent finds irksome and interesting – the up and downsides of the job. Note the demands on the skills, training and knowledge of the incumbent and what is referred up and down. Talk over your findings with the departmental manager and, when back in the office, check with other records such as job descriptions in that department or of similar jobs performed elsewhere in the organization. If they are to hand look at records of 'exit interviews' (i.e. notes made when someone is leaving a similar job) and job/performance reviews. All of these have a story to tell and help to form an accurate, working picture of the job, turning a theoretical concept into a practical reality.

The 'write-up' should be done while this information is still fresh; further facts can be added later if not immediately available. Quantifiable data (such as product runs; product lines; time needed to re-tool; wastage or spoiled merchandise; productivity; downtime etc.) is especially valuable both to measure the job and to describe it later to possible candidates. For a traineeship the Instructors can give useful information about learning rates, the range of tasks to be learnt, mental and physical dexterity, skills required and so on. Departmental staff turnover and sickness records yield clues as to morale and working conditions as well as other things. Armed with this information, you can now analyse the job.

Job analysis

This term is often used to cover both Job Description and Job Analysis, but in practice they are two separate procedures – or should be. The facts have to be obtained before they can be analysed; and facts are facts, analysis is judgemental. If the description is in narrative form, the analysis should be systematic and provide answers to specific questions (it is often best written in 'boxes').

The precise format used is of less importance than the content. The analysis can usefully be subdivided into five areas:

Organizational position
Principal tasks
Resources
Personal factors
Personnel factors.

Organizational position. This should state the title of the person to whom the incumbent is responsible, the location of the job and principal working relationships. Reference can be made to an organization chart. 'Dotted line' relations (i.e. in a matrix-style organization, where job performance and functional responsibilities are split) should be clearly defined.

Principal tasks. Only the key aspects or duties/responsibilities should be stated and these in terms of end result rather than a long list of detailed tasks. The latter are bound to change. It should admit of a fair degree of flexibility but not be too wide open. 'Carry out such tasks as may be determined by the Head of Department' may give management a lot of scope but will be too ill defined for most people and open to abuse. Likewise, anything which clearly has a built-in obsolescence should be avoided. 'Working with the Computer Analysts to write such computer programmes as are required within the Management Information System currently in use' is better than specifying computer languages, computer hardware and current applications. If an umbrella clause is needed – and it often is – then it should define acceptable limits and state 'as may be agreed within the skills and competences of a professionally trained xyz'. It is better to concentrate on the key tasks and insert a few umbrella clauses than to try to cover every eventuality.

Resources are the tools available to do the job and can usefully be listed under three headings. *Equipment* – a brief description of the main equipment in current use; add a phrase like 'and its replacement in due course'. *Money* – show capital and revenue budgets separately and say something like 'as are agreed from time to time (normally annually in March)'. You could add 'to make proposals for inclusion in the annual business plan and to operate within the budget constraints ultimately agreed by the Management Committee' etc. *People* – if the job is a supervisory one either on an attachment or permanent basis, the typical number and range of skilled people available should be shown (with scope to change over time). Resources may sometimes be external; a purchasing manager may be empowered to place sub-contract manufacturing and, in conjunction with the production engineers, monitor performance including off-site inspection and rejection of work not up to specification.

Personal factors are the levels and range of skills required, knowledge (usually in terms of professional or academic qualifications), depth of experience (e.g. managing a sales team in the Far East with personal experience in at least one major territory) for the fully trained incumbent. It should avoid 'in-company' type knowledge unless this is axiomatic to the performance of the job; in that case, state how long it will take an intelligent newcomer to obtain this knowledge. Refer also to travel, (defined by areas/length of time away from base etc), if this is a feature of the job, unsocial hours or other domestic disturbance (home entertainment of overseas customers or staff), unusual pressures such as seasonal deadlines; onerous, critical decisions. Work- and people-generated pressures should be separated, as some find the one easier to cope with than the other.

Personnel factors can be broken down into, for example, three areas: scope for training and development; scope for using the job flexibly (i.e. flexitime working, job sharing, home working, etc.), scope for using the job as a training stage or for an older person close to retirement. Finally, you should describe the job grade and rating on pay scales, including reference to bonus arrangements.

When drafted, the description and analysis should be discussed in detail with the departmental manager or superior for accuracy, omissions etc. It is very important that this is done thoroughly as it will form the basis of all that follows. Inadequate attention at this stage is a prime source of revenue for the recruitment consultants!

The person specification

Job analysis provides the basic material for drawing up a person specification. The shape of the ideal person is already starting to emerge. The danger is that idealism flies in the face of reality: we have to recruit in the real world. The person specification should be based on the absolute minimum requirements needed to perform the job satisfactorily (after an initial training period, if necessary). These requirements should be clearly separated from the 'desirable' qualities we should like to see but which depend largely on market conditions. Far too many person specifications are over-idealized or myopic and stem from looking through the wrong end of the telescope. Employment is a double-sided contract between a willing candidate and a prospective employer. Far too many able and willing candidates are rejected out of hand through sheer prejudice. This is the prime cause of so much discrimination. It has taken decades of campaigning and legislation for many employers to accept that women can do a very wide range of jobs just as effectively as their male counterparts. The same is true of racial minorities and older people.

The recruiter needs to be aware of current legislation in this area (the Department of Employment is a ready source of free advice and advisory leaflets, which every personnel department should keep up to date; the Institute of Personnel Management also issues regular guidelines, codes of conduct and considered articles on current legislation and good practice which are available to members – and to Non-Members at modest charges). It is helpful to think of specific people we know doing similar jobs to keep our feet on the ground. There are plenty of people with minimum professional or academic qualifications holding down key senior appointments; youngsters with little experience showing a maturity of judgement often lacking in an older person; older people with more enterprise, drive and energy than people half their age. To pitch the person specification at too high a level is a sheer waste of time and effort. Likewise, if you are adamant that a job can only be filled acceptably by someone within the company or industry, why waste time and frustrate everyone concerned just to prove you are right?

It is important that the person specification is drawn up in terms that are quantifiable and can be matched with measurable skills and attributes in candidates. It was the late Professor Alec Rodger who first expressed this many years ago: 'If matching is to be done satisfactorily, the requirements of an occupation (or job) must be described in the same terms as the attributes of people who are being considered for it.' This has given rise to the famous Seven Point Plan – later reduced to five by T. Munro Fraser:

Seven Point Plan	*Five Point Plan*
Physical make-up	Impact on other people
Attainments	Qualifications
General Intelligence	Brains and abilities
Specialized aptitudes	Motivation
Interests	Adjustment
Disposition	
Circumstances	

These are then listed as 'essential' and 'desirable' attributes along with any major 'contra indications' (i.e. attributes which would disqualify someone even though all other criteria are satisfied). Using these seven or five headings as guidelines the person specification can then be drawn up.

Physical make-up (or impact on other people)

Don't describe the obvious but concentrate on key issues. If physique and strength, stretch or reach, hand dexterity or keen vision, is vital, say so and specify in medical terms or by reference to known factors in the job (e.g. 'Must be able to carry loads up to 50kg'; 'to reach shelves 1.75m high'; 'to distinguish between grey and green on components 3mm across'; etc.). A salesperson or manager has to interact with and influence specific types of people, so describe them in simple terms (e.g. purchasing staff in major motor manufacturers; primary school teachers; a department of 50–100 skilled and semi-skilled operatives; and so on).

Attainments (or qualifications)

These are the minimum professional, academic or trade skills needed to do the job and can be described in terms of university degrees, GCSEs, trade qualifications or simply experience (e.g.

'Need to have sold similar products throughout France, Germany and Italy'; 'have managed a mixed-tribe labour force of semi-skilled workers in West Africa'; 'can demonstrate WP skills using WP50 or WordStar'.

General intelligence (or brains and abilities)

The five point plan combines several of the seven point factors, but this should be readily apparent. By 'general intelligence' is meant the ability to achieve scores of defined levels in intelligence tests (e.g. Grade A on all parts of AH5, university norms) or by reference to a normative group ('the level of intelligence displayed by sixth formers'); or the ability to learn new skills within a specified time. Try not to guess but use a normative measure wherever possible. To use an analogy with cars, this is the rating of the engine and the previous factor the gearing and demonstrated performance.

Specialized aptitudes

Commonly we call this 'flair' and it is best described in terms of abilities: thinking in three dimensions, sensitive colour matching, understanding and correcting electronic faults, or playing a sport to national team level etc. These can be tested using psychometrics e.g. the Engineering Apprenticeship test battery, by examining work samples or probing past experience. They are unusual skills and generally have a high visibility. Most people will prefer to think in terms of personality, but both plans aim to make us think in objective terms and try to suppress the amateur psychologist tendency in most recruiters.

Interests

These are underlying preferences for courses of action such as report writing, practical work, overseas travel, innovation, outdoor work, face-to-face contacts, negotiating etc.

Disposition

Friendly, cold, hostile, accommodating, easy-going, critical etc.

Motivation

This is one aspect of Interests; motivation springs from one's need for money, power, influence, intellectual excellence, doing one's best for one's family or the team etc. If this source of motivation can be aligned with a job, the individual is more likely to succeed.

Adjustment

This is a tricky one; we know what we mean by the term, but it is difficult to describe. Maturity of judgement and behaviour, the ability to establish friendships and relationships with a wide range of people, responsible behaviour, the ability to withstand the 'slings and arrows of outrageous fortune' without being bowled over, all spring to mind. If maturity is vital, note it; if the position is going to generate stress, note its likely source (e.g. 'must be able to make rapid decisions if apparatus breaks down'; 'must be able to keep temper even when provoked').

Circumstances

This refers to the sensitive area of home life. If the job involves entertaining overseas customers at home, this must be noted and the facilities must exist. This is particularly important if the incumbent's partner will be involved too. If the job entails long periods of absence from home, it cannot be ignored – though if things are known to be difficult it is possible that alternative arrangements may be made. Conversely, a partner's linguistic skills may be a great asset.

If you draw up the person specification in this way, it is readily seen that people and jobs *can* be described in identical terms which make assessment so much easier and more accurate.

The people market

Many recruitment exercises fail because no-one has asked two basic questions: Do the candidates exist (and, if so, where are they?)? And what are our chances of attracting anyone to this job? If the candidates do not exist (as you have described them) or cannot be attracted to your area, or if your rates/conditions/ company reputation are bad, this must be faced *before* going to the marketplace. It is not difficult to carry out some limited market research into the people market. The local Department of Employment, other local employers, a word with others in the company who have been recruiting recently, your own records, the recruitment advertising agency you use, comment in the news-papers or the professional and business press – the information is readily to hand. Executive search companies employ researchers specifically for this purpose; before they attempt to approach anyone they spend time evaluating the candidate market (where precisely are they? What are the chances that they will respond positively to our approach?).

Armed with this information, recruiters can analyse the need from first principles.

Do we need to recruit at all?

If the candidate has to come from within, then internal advertising may be the answer. If you know there is no-one available, the job has to be recast – perhaps certain tasks can be reallocated or the job simplified in some way. If the job is only temporary, a temporary employee may be the answer. If the job has been created to suit the whim of some senior executive, perhaps he or she can be persuaded to think again!

Can we attract anyone?

If the results of the research enquiries suggest that, for whatever reason, the company cannot attract anyone suitable, then it is 'back to the drawing board'. There are many possible solutions. The specification may be flexible enough to permit modification. Enhancing the job (in seniority or scope) may make it more attractive. Money or the reward package may be the problem.

Could the job be done at another office or from home? Can the contract be modified in another way – for example, by a longer notice period to reassure candidates?

Should the job be filled in some other way?

The job could be filled by a succession of trainees who may be persuaded to put up with uncongenial conditions for, say, 6 months to gain experience or 'exposure' to top management. The job may be considered 'dead-end' but may appeal for that very reason to someone approaching retirement who is not looking for further promotion. Or to someone looking for a short-term stint prior to maternity leave. Or to someone in failing health whose occasional absence might not be critical. It is surprising what can be done when the need arises!

The training option

Some jobs can be used as training slots on a more permanent basis; for Government-aided schemes such as YTS or for the company's own apprentices/trainees, or to help older people coming back to work or young employees in need of experience. Junior doctors are a good case in point. Too often the training option is dismissed because extra supervision may be needed, but this can be offset by the high calibre of trainee. Finally, if it is not possible to recruit someone externally, the job may be filled by training up an existing employee.

Human resource planning

It was once popular in larger companies to employ specialist statisticians who would work closely with corporate planners in forecasting longer-term people needs (the job of the training and management development people was to put these plans into effect). At the time of writing, many of these specialists have been absorbed into other jobs. During a recession, such a person seems a luxury few can afford. Yet if the appointment is a luxury, the work is vital. Much training activity is based on longer-term projections, and recruiters too need to know of such plans. If manufacturing methods are to change radically; if new products are to be introduced and old ones phased out; if offices are to be relocated or closed; if major expansions – or contractions – are planned, recruitment can be re-phased. There may be time to train up more school leavers, now may be the moment to start up training in skills such as languages. Recruiting the ready-made specialist is always expensive; trainees are more plentiful, cheaper and generally stay longer.

Human resource planning need not be complex and it uses many of the skills and techniques used in other kinds of planning. It starts with a stock-taking of existing resources by level of skills, age, likely availability (bearing in mind retirement, turnover statistics by occupation/age, those already under training etc). The results can be drawn up on graph paper and plotted against forecast requirements. The gaps will need to be filled by trainees or internal/external recruitment. This can only yield probabilities, since employment is dynamic and can change dramatically due to external, unforeseen factors – but that is no excuse for ignoring those areas under one's control. The desperate dearth of certain grades of employees and the glut of others along with the comparatively low level of training in the UK are largely due to 'short-termism' and the lack of such planning.

Legal requirements should also be considered. The workforce, for example, has to reflect ethnic population patterns. Equal opportunities must be given to men and women; attempts deliberately to circumvent this can result in heavy penalties. Directives from the European Commission have increasingly to be taken into account in these areas, and in others such as payments to part-timers, hours worked, employment of minors, health and safety and so on. What is certain is that there is pressure to promote 'best practice' throughout the EC and to ensure true competition, which will undoubtedly affect the whole area of employment.

Whatever the plans, they will need to be examined at regular intervals – probably quarterly – since, as with financial forecasting, so much can happen in a short time. Recording needs to be kept simple and easily comprehensible, so that up-dating is not a tremendous and time-consuming chore – a sure recipe for neglect! If the company's plans affect external bodies such as local colleges, schools or universities regularly used as a source of recruits, liaison is both sensible and good manners; it is no use blaming the education system if the 'powers that be' are not kept in the picture.

A practical example

1 The personnel manager is notified that the records clerk in the drawing office (DO) has handed in her notice because she is leaving the district.

2 He arranges to discuss the job with:
the drawing office manager
the woman's section leader
the woman herself.

3 The manager can only spare five minutes. She says the clerk is a pleasant woman and she is sorry to see her go. She hopes the replacement will be a stayer because it is important to have continuity on records. She thinks everything has gone smoothly lately on records but is not in touch with the details of the job.

4 The section leader provides an abundance of comment and information. He lists the records maintained by the clerk, who runs a type of computerized library system for recording details of many thousands of drawings and issuing and retrieving prints. He estimates the number of drawings issued daily; the enquiries received by telephone, the time spent on searching the files and records. He takes the personnel manager to watch the woman at work with her cabinets, computer and telephone at the end of the DO. She is carefully entering identification details from a batch of new drawings on to microfiche records. As she works, she is interrupted three times by telephone enquiries about tooling and pattern numbers. These she answers by referring to a mini-computer on her desk. One of the draughtsmen comes to her desk with a query. She answers him and then they chat casually for some minutes. She continues to enter details on her machine while talking. The personnel manager examines some of the entries she has made, notes the complexity of the computerized records, notes also the height and extent of the suspension files which occupy one

wall of the DO and notes the calm and concentration of the clerk.

5   Later, the personnel manager sees the records clerk privately to discuss her reasons for leaving and to learn more about the job, her attitude to it and her attitude to the company. He asks her what parts of the job she found difficult to learn, what she will be most glad to get away from when she leaves. He gets examples of the sorts of question she receives by telephone and finds that she uses her memory a good deal, has devised a way of classifying some types of information regularly needed by adding extra signals to the computer records, and prepares a monthly print out for the cost accountant listing all tools reported broken or re-ordered. (This was not mentioned by the section leader.) He then goes on to talk about the district she is moving to. He gains the impression that she has enjoyed her work which has brought her into contact with many departments and that she is sorry to be leaving.

6   There are no records in the personnel department about this job. It appears to have grown up around the woman who was recruited four and a half years ago as a school-leaver. Initially employed on tracing (she had done mechanical drawing at school and had asked for training as a draughtswoman), she was given responsibility for records when they were reorganized two years ago.

7   The personnel manager drafts a job description, carries out his job analysis and then prepares a person specification. These drafts may be modified in a final talk with the section leader and drawing office manager, and will then serve as the yardstick by which he will seek and assess candidates for the job.

Job description

Title Records Clerk
Department Drawing Office
Accountable to Section Leader (Designs)
Supporting staff None
Number employed on this work 1
Replacement available None

Position from which candidates for this position might come DO trainees

Avenues of promotion/transfer from this position Higher grade clerical work

1 *Purpose and objects of work*

Ensures that all drawings and prints in current use can be identified and located, that only up to date drawings are in use; that dimensions of tools and patterns in use can be checked centrally; that records are kept of tool breakages for costing purposes.

2 *Activities*

(a) Issues classification numebrs for all new drawings and enters details on to mini-computer records.

(b) Enters dates and modification details to records when drawings are modified. Destroys all unmodified prints.

(c) Files drawings and spare prints in appropriate lateral files.

(d) Maintains register of re-ordered tools and prepares monthly print out for the cost office.

(e) Answers queries from production departments, DO staff, cost office, relating to modifications in progress, tool and pattern identification numbers, location of prints.

(f) Requisitions new microfiches and issues prints to works departments noting dates and quantities issued.

(g) Regularly reviews files for obsolete records. Informs section leader when additional filing capacity is required.

3 *Circumstances*

(a) Work subject to continuous interruption by telephone and by personal enquirers.

(b) Due to growth of business, volume of work increasing monthly. Two new suspension filing cabinets added recently.

(c) Estimated number of queries per day: 50
New drawings registered daily: 15 (average)
Drawings issued daily: variable. Builds up to peaks when new lines are being introduced.

(d) Most time spent satisfying queries. These often involve searching records and telephoning other departments.

(e) Main difficulty is concentration in spite of interruptions.

Work demands accuracy, computer literacy, a liking for
routine, a helpful disposition and an easy social manner.

Job analysis

Personal requirements
Educational and vocational knowledge No qualifications essential.
Good school record needed as evidence of application, concentration and intelligence (see details below).
Experience of dealing with engineering drawings and ability to
distinguish main features is desirable.
Experience Minimum age about 18. Prior experience of record
keeping essential. Previous experience of working with computers would be valuable. Ideal experience would be in a production scheduling or sales administration office of an engineering works, or as a trainee in a drawing office for at least a year
after leaving school.
Physical effort and skill Some reaching into tall cabinets. Minimum height about 1m 60. Work is mainly sedentary.
Adaptability and concentration Routine work, subject to interruptions, requiring close concentration.
Intelligence No complex problems to solve. Above average intelligence would be unsuitable.
Disposition and temperament Critical requirements are a helpful, patient disposition and a liking for routine work involving
accuracy. Must not be shy. A friendly and brisk manner is
appropriate.

Responsibilities
Controls no staff. Takes no decisions affecting others.
Contacts are informal and with drawing office personnel, super-
visors, departmental heads and computer services department.
No external contacts.
Confidential information as for all DO staff.
Assets and materials Responsible for care and safe custody of
essential records.

Special features
Working conditions Pleasant newly-built office. Brisk and
friendly atmosphere.

Difficulties Growing volume of work and enquiries.
Consequence of error Inaccuracies and omissions by the record clerk could result in delays to manufacture or even manufacture of obsolete parts.
Supervision received Main check is absence of complaints. No direct supervision possible because of degree of detail.
Satisfaction In solving queries and providing an efficient service – in range of contacts within the company.
Conditions of service Weekly staff terms. Job graded as C with merit increments. Current salary £xx at age 20.

The person specification

Physical make-up	Minimum height 1m 60
	Pleasant appearance
	Brisk, clear speech, free from impediments
Attainments	Essential to have evidence of application, concentration and capacity for detailed work.
	Desirable to have some knowledge of technical drawing and of engineering terms.
	Education should reflect academic or technical bias e.g. technical drawing. Four O Levels or the equivalent previous experience of record keeping in technical office or library is essential.
	Experience of working with engineering drawings is desirable.
	Computer keyboard skills desirable.
General intelligence	Brisk reactions and an accurate memory are needed rather than ability to solve complex problems.
Specialized aptitudes	Neat, quick and accurate at clerical work.
Interests	Practical and social.
Disposition	Self-reliant, helpful, friendly.
Circumstances	A person who is likely to stay for at least three years is preferred.
Contra-indications	Obvious shyness or a grasshopper mentality.

Possible sources
>Internal –Transfer from production, sales, planning or DO?
>External –DoE? YTS? Advertise?

2

Attracting the right candidates

Summary

No amount of interviewing will turn unsuitable applicants into good candidates. This stage needs care and a knowledge of the marketplace. Knowing how the group of people you want to attract go about finding a new job; where they are and what will appeal to them is vital. An analysis of current personnel records will yield clues (providing past trends are a true guide to today's marketplace), as will a study of local and national newspapers, trade journals and local radio. There is plenty of external advice available: the DoE, local employment agencies, trade union local officials, local employers' organizations and a whole raft of consultants.

Recruitment advertising is a specialist skill available at no cost from a specialist recruitment advertising agency. Taking their advice can save literally thousands of pounds. Those who lack the time or the expertise are well advised to go to an agency/consultancy with proven, relevant skills.

Good PR can also help. All employers soon acquire a local reputation as an employer – for good or bad. A good reputation will lead to a steady flow of casual applications from the best local people. This can extend to local schools, colleges, universities, training organizations and trade unions. Personal recommendation from someone whose judgement is known to be sound can be invaluable.

There is plenty of help available. A brief guide to consultants – and how to assess them – appears on pages 45–6.

Finding suitable candidates

In good times and bad 'good candidates' are hard to find. This is partly due to the pace of change and the seemingly perpetual imbalance between supply and demand; and partly to poor job analysis and inadequate knowledge of the outside people market which leads many employers to seek the impossible and rush into print before coolly weighing up the situation.

Few recruitment 'problems' are insoluble, given common sense and some flexibility. Suitable candidates generally do exist and can be attracted, however tough the assignment. The secret lies in an understanding of the marketplace:

* Where are they?
* How can they be contacted?
* Can we attract them?

Where are they?

Candidates can be found in groups or as individuals. In some industries, teams stick together (e.g. construction). In a somewhat nomadic way of life, managers and foremen attract personal loyalty; recruit the gaffer and a whole team follows at little or no expense! Other groups can be found in companies undergoing change (redeployment, redundancy due to changing technology or poor management, takeover, merger etc). School leavers and others leaving full-time education or a recognized training course can be easily identified. The DoE is generally aware of pockets of unemployment or likely change. Sometimes these pockets are overseas. Many West Africans and West Indians were recruited in the 1950's by the railways, and Italians – on 2-year contracts – by the brick makers and some foundries; computer programmers are currently coming from the Irish Republic; many nurses come from Northern Ireland and many Scottish engineers man overseas installations. Some industries are local – shoemaking, glassmaking, steelmaking, textiles, shipbuilding etc – so while skilled tradespeople are readily found in these areas, they may be impossible to find elsewhere and not willing to move. Although there are pockets of electronic engineers in many parts of the country, many of these are highly specialized and employed in small companies; the same is true of computer personnel. In many other occupations – such as financial services, retail, local government, transport etc – employers are more widely and evenly spread. In general, the more senior the appointment the more widely scattered are the candidates. Of course, there are the exceptions; the main advertising agencies are grouped in the West End; most merchant bankers and international financiers are to be found in the City; and many company HQ staff have relocated to Scotland or the North East. These, however, have mostly to be considered as individuals when planning a recruitment campaign, especially if they are currently based outside this country.

How can they be contacted?

Job-seeking habits are fairly strongly established in the UK culture and change is slow and easily charted. There has been much experimentation by employers in recent years – notably recruitment fairs – but many of the old traditions persist. Social class, local tradition, level of appointment and communication channel availability all have a bearing. The different kinds of candidate can be broadly classified as follows:

School/college/university leavers will be guided by academic staff and parents. Careers/appointments services provide some guidance and literature, but a significant number still tend to follow in parental footsteps or those of family friends. The experience of last year's students will tend to sway opinions. The lower the intellectual level and the social class, the more localized the horizons will be (this may change later). Ethnic minorities often display their own variations and preferences for certain occupations; the Irish are attracted to the construction industry, the Scots to accountancy and engineering, the Welsh to teaching, Pakistanis to retail business, Italians to the restaurant and hotel business, and so on. One assumes that the opening of the European market will tend over time to extend this pattern further.

Production staff. Many of these are more concerned with the locality than the precise job and so are readily retrained. Skilled people may be more adventurous and travel further. The local employment office, a notice at the factory gate, the local press and radio, local cinema and other employees are all effective vehicles for communicating job opportunities. The relevant trade unions can also be helpful, though many employers fear the return of restrictive practices and union control (as was common among printers and dockers until recently).

Office staff. The dividing line between office/shop/junior clerical staff and factory operatives is receding and much the same patterns can be discerned. Perhaps there is still more emphasis on local press and radio advertising and word of mouth.

Senior office staff like secretaries, computer programmers, accountancy assistants, local government junior executive staff and so on mostly respond to advertisements in local and regional press or radio or prefer to go through a local, specialist agency. Word of mouth can be important too.

Non-professional, technical staff will tend to look further afield and be prepared to commute longer distances, though they will prefer to remain within their native region.

Technicians vary widely and comprise laboratory assistants, draughtsmen and women, service engineers and that broad band of people who fall just short of true professional status. They are widely scattered geographically and so they look to national and local advertising as well as the appropriate trade and professional journals. They are too hard to identify and too far down within the organization for executive search techniques to be used.

Professionally qualified staff. Although there are regional variations, most categories are nationally distributed and often international. Traditionally, this group was reached through the national 'quality' press and professional journals. Trade fairs have been successful for the more junior people here and overseas. Young, newly qualified accountants are frequently recruited from the large firms of auditors quite openly since there is mutual benefit. Many are recruited through firms of recruitment consultants who may also build registers of the more senior and experienced people. Those from the business schools can be recruited in the same way as young graduates.

Senior management/top professionals in 1991 will be earning in excess of £35,000 p.a. Although spread nationally – and even internationally, especially within the EEC – they can be effectively targeted and many will respond to national and professional advertising. The very top group – those earning over £75,000 p.a. in 1991 – are usually approached directly through a third party and it was for this group that executive search was first established.

Recruitment advertising

Press, radio and TV recruitment advertising has become a new profession during the past 35 years initially because of full employment, higher literacy and social mobility. The grammar schools produced a new breed of technicians and professionals who could not rely on the old family contacts and introductions which favoured the products of public schools. Easier travel and higher salaries meant that relocation was accepted, especially by those setting out to build their career with the larger companies. Even the Civil Service soon began to top up its 'examination-entry' grades by taking in selected specialists with outside knowledge and experience.

As firms of all kinds felt the need to tap this new source of recruits, they began to vie with each other and compete openly through recruitment drives in schools, colleges and the universities and through press advertising. At first this was ignored or disdained by the larger advertising agencies, who did not recognize the enormous potential and could still only think in terms of lineage announcements handled by the most junior staff. Specialist agencies and consultancies rapidly 'cut their teeth' in the 1960s and 1970s and have established a whole new science/art form. Costs have risen astronomically; advertisers who could afford to take space in three or four national newspapers plus one or two journals and to re-advertise if necessary in the early 1960s have to spend an equivalent amount on one prominent advertisement in a national newspaper today. The penalty for inefficient advertising is considerable.

The services of an advertising agency are usually free as they obtain a discount from the media owner which usually covers their costs. The good agency should provide:

- Advice on the candidate market
- Advice on the selection of media
- Advice on copy or a copy-writing service
- A design service including graphics
- Production, purchasing, proof-reading
- Confirmation of appearance

Many also provide brochure writing and production, posters, the organization of recruitment campaigns (including venues), translation into other languages, reply vetting, market research and so on. Some have much better facilities and better informed staff than others, but the large national agency charges no more than the small local firm. Choice of agency will depend on the level and speed of response as much as on copy-writing and design skills. The quality of the 'account executive' (the immediate contact point) is of paramount importance. Many are ex-personnel professionals who have acquired the relevant skills or are backed by skilled advertisers; others are 'slick messenger boys' who leave the company to do all the copywriting, market research and so on.

Planning

Whether for a single advertisement or a sustained campaign, careful planning is important. It is quite possible to produce either a large or a compact response, depending on the media coverage, the number of possible candidates, the budget and the looseness or tightness of the candidate specification. If large numbers are required (e.g. trainees or staff for a new office or factory), the budget can be larger, allowing for some preliminary testing or market research. If the demand is for a single individual, a dozen suitable candidates are ample – any more will just add unnecessarily to the cost and those rejected without interview may then be reluctant to reapply when a more suitable job is advertised.

Timing is also important. Certain publications have recruitment features on certain days; custom varies between countries so that Saturday is best in one, Sunday in another, an evening paper in a third. Not all countries have effective national publications, so the regional press or weeklies may be preferred. And so on. Media planning can be a nightmare to the uninitiated; the agency should provide this as part of the package. An advertisement needs to appear when candidates can easily respond – which is why weekends are often preferred – or, if replies are by telephone, when the office is properly manned. To advertise and then go away is futile if candidates want to talk over their suitability. Good candidates are always in short supply and advertising should screen out the unsuitable and facilitate the application of the suitable. The overall aim is to achieve a compact field of suitable, well-motivated people who are willing to undergo the trauma of selection because they want the job so badly!

Wording/design

The simplicity of good advertising 'copy' is deceptive and hides the hours spent trying to make the optimum use of expensive space. The wording and design of a recruitment advertisement is quite unlike that for product advertising. The latter depends on repetition, brand image and brand awareness; it never has to compete with a rival product on the same page. The recruitment advertisement is jostling for attention among perhaps 10 pages of competing advertisements. It is generally a 'one-off' and must be made to work first time. The company may have a brand image which can be usefully harnessed, but this must be carefully handled. Too frequent, random advertising suggests high turnover or indecisive management, whereas a sustained, planned build-up at a new facility can be attractive.

The wording falls into four main sections:

heading
sub-heads
body copy
action message.

The heading has to have instant appeal to the right candidates rapidly scanning those 10 or more pages. It flags the subject and induces the reader to read further. The skills of the newspaper editor are worth studying carefully. A heading may be a single word like 'War!' or a short sentence: 'At last – we've won the Ashes!' *The sub-head* then reinforces or modifies the heading: 'Open rebellion among tribal chiefs' or 'Australia collapse on 85 all out'. The reader may study the rest of the article or move on. Likewise with a job advertisement. 'Director' may have wide appeal; 'new hi-tech facility' will narrow the field. The headline may present a gimmick or a challenge such as 'Ninety-nine accountants out of a hundred wouldn't look at this job', and the sub-head an enticing inducement like 'quality car'. More time will be usually spent on the heading and sub-head than on all the rest of the copy.

The body copy usually tells the reader something about the employer, the job, the requirements and the terms offered. Often the first sentence (as in an editorial) encapsulates the essence of the story or the appeal: 'This is an opportunity for an experienced laser-physicist to set up a new research facility backed by a major international engineering concern.' It starts to screen out the unsuitable and (hopefully) to attract someone casually keeping an eye on the job advertisements for an exciting new opportunity. By selective use of facts or figures the reader's interest is enhanced or modified as the background, the task to be done, where the job fits into the hierarchy and the resources available are all sketched in. The next paragraph usually spells out the key require-ments (beware of anything that smacks of discrimination) set out in the job analysis, and is followed by a brief summary of the terms offered. The quality of this copy will determine the quality of the response; by carefully selecting and presenting the facts the candidate wants to know (*not* vague company bombast) the selection process can meaningfully begin. Research has shown time and again that candidates do not like gimmicks; that they take the business of job change very seriously; that they want facts – especially salary – and that the whole must form 'a viable proposition'. In highly competitive markets anything less will lead to a nil response.

The action message spells out how candidates should respond. 'Please write fully to show your suitability with examples of recent work, at least three references and a recent photograph' will, needless to say, draw a smaller response than 'Ring Jo Johnson on 081 234 5678 any time for further information.' The action demanded should be suited to the job-seeking habits of candi-dates. Secretaries may be asked to phone, so that telephone manner and voice can be assessed – this is a fair sample of the work to be done. The workman likes to turn up at the factory dressed ready for work early in the day. The model wants time to dress and have a hair-do. Some expect to be asked to fill in an application blank, while others will send an example of recent work like a report, design or academic paper as well as a c.v. (curriculum vitae or life history). If linguistic skill is required, evidence such as a c.v. in French may be requested. Unsuitable candidates may think this an unreasonable demand, but it reveals your seriousness of intent to the people who count.

Design

There are three aspects of design relevant to recruitment advertisements:

House style
Typography
Illustration

House style is comparable to brand image in product advertising. By using, say, a similar design style in overall appearance (border, typeface, illustration, company logo, lay-out, overall shape), a company's advertisements can be instantly recognized. This can also project a general image that will enhance other advertisements (caring, generous, interesting jobs, career scope, mobility, people-orientated, enterprising etc). Companies in the public eye will often link product and recruitment advertising in this way.

Typography is the choice of typeface and use of space. An advertisement should be readable as well as legible – even in the lineage columns – and good typographical design can greatly enhance the visual appeal of an advertisement. Unlike the product advertisement which relies heavily on illustrations, the recruitment advertisement often depends entirely on typography for its visual appeal. There is a very wide range of typefaces and sizes available, although advertisements set by the publication itself are restricted to the faces and sizes held by the printer, which are not always known in advance. While this is cheaper (publishers, unlike advertising agencies, do not charge for 'production'), one can be a hostage to fortune; the £100 spent on 'having it set' can be money well spent.

Illustration. Photographs and drawings, sometimes in colour, can be used merely as part of a house style or to link product with recruitment advertising. Yet a carefully selected photograph or drawing can 'speak volumes' and help to attract the interest of suitable candidates. Agencies, of course, charge for this work but will work to a budget. Freelance artists, such as well-known cartoonists, may also be used.

Media selection

The temptation is always to go for the most popular – and therefore the most expensive – national newspaper, but choice of medium should be based entirely on the readership habits of the target audience *when looking to change their job*. Many publications are read widely for general interest but are useless for recruitment purposes. Unfortunately publications rarely give 'page traffic' data (i.e. what percentage of their readers look at specific pages or sections) and refuse to accept that readership data produced for more lucrative product marketing is irrelevant for recruitment purposes. A few agencies keep data relating to response to previous advertisements and any company which advertises frequently is wise to do so. A card file with a copy of the advertisement pasted on one side and response figures on the other (number of replies; interviewed; offered jobs; appointed) is all that is necessary. Questioning current staff and interviewees can also produce useful data. Newspapers are said to have a 'short shelf life' because they change daily, though the week-end press may be kept a little longer. Journals are often kept for longer periods and circulated among specialist staff. On the face of it these should be ideal, but often they have no recruitment tradition and are read very selectively and so are unreliable. Others are very well worthwhile.

The lineage columns (so called because space is sold by the line instead of by the column centimetre or fraction of a page) are popular with many people but rarely read by professional or 'higher grade' staff. For example, the classified lineage columns of the London *Evening Standard* carry hundreds of advertisements (more accurately announcements) daily for drivers, waitresses, hairdressers, gardeners, clerical staff and so on; they are cheap and often very effective. Space can be bought 'semi-display', allowing for a heading and a separate paragraph or two which is still charged at the lineage rate.

Radio, TV and cinema advertising have the advantage that, like product advertising, they do not compete for attention directly. You buy time according to potential audience (based on research) and are charged for segments of time at peak or off-peak hours in particular areas of distribution. These advertisements have to be professionally produced and, if filming is involved, can be very costly. The major TV networks are rarely used, partly on grounds of cost and partly because response can be overwhelming. Off-peak TV has been used in the smaller regions as a pointer to a national press advertisement the next day, and more often for large-scale recruitment (e.g. for the armed services, nursing etc). Local radio is much cheaper and competes effectively with the local press for jobs up to the technician level. Housewives and the unemployed are the main targets during the day; school leavers later; employed people during meal breaks, while travelling to and from work and during evenings and weekends. Cinema advertising is usually used for large-scale recruitment especially among young people – for retail store staff, apprenticeships and so on. If production is not done professionally the result is likely to be counter-productive. Advertising agencies are the answer.

External support services

Summary

There is a wide range of external support services available to cover most contingencies. Consultancies will handle the complete campaign or significant parts of it at every level of need. Some will be costly but may still be cheaper than using expensive executive time and high office overheads; they may also save thousands of pounds by preventing a bad appointment. The Department of Employment provides an efficient local service for advice; displays of vacancies; careers, youth and adult training and retraining schemes, and information on those soon to be available. Their advisory service covers every aspect of employment (including recruitment) and is useful to professionals as well as to generalist managers. Most, if not all, services are free at the time of writing.

Employment agencies

These act on behalf of both employers and candidates, though they only make a charge to the employer (by law they cannot charge both). They are to be found all over the UK and vary widely since they target different segments of the local population. The largest are run by the Department of Employment; though often regarded as 'down market', Job Shops are professionally run by well-trained staff and cover the complete spectrum of employment. However, now that the former PER (Professional and Executive Register) has been sold, the Job Shops tend to concentrate on 'lower-level' appointments, school leavers and attempts to help the unemployed get back to work through counselling and retraining schemes.

Many government-sponsored schemes are available to help people retrain – especially mothers who, after a period of absence, wish to return to paid employment but feel the need for a refresher course. The DoE provides advice and guidance on legal requirements such as Contract of Employment Acts, equal opportunities, discrimination, redundancy, the employment of ex-offenders, quota requirements (for disabled staff), employment of foreigners and so on. The Department is able to locate pockets of unemployment and help employers with interviewing arrangements. They can also advise on local rates of pay.

Private employment agencies have to be licensed by the DoE; this also applies to consultancies which, strictly speaking, do not operate in the same way. In general, the staff of local, private employment agencies are not so well qualified, though some do employ personnel professionals. Theirs is essentially a quick, commercial service geared to a rapid turnover of candidates. The advice they give will be market-related. Sometimes they will advertise vacancies free and charge on a 'no appointment, no fee' basis. Some specialize – secretaries or legal staff, for example – others take what comes, though usually they handle 'staff' rather than 'shopfloor' appointments.

Candidate registers

Many employment agencies and consultancies maintain a register of people interested in changing their job. Some deliberately build up a register by advertising; others charge candidates for a regular mass mailing (in other words, it can work both ways: the former charge an employer for a placement, the latter are free). On the face of it this is a quick and relatively cheap way of finding out who is available and what pay they are looking for. In practice, unless the register is constantly topped up with a large number of new candidates, there is insufficient choice and the 'good' people have gone before the register is circulated. The Data Protection Act also places constraints on would-be register compilers that some find costly (e.g. the need constantly to update data; ensuring candidates are content with the wording of their entry and so on). This means that the use of registers is changing to 'doing a file search' (i.e. seeking to match a candidate profile with a job specification, probably by computers). However, people and jobs admit of infinite variations and exact matching is often extremely difficult; while in theory jobs can be adapted to suit individuals, this is rare in reality. Many candidates today circulate their c.v. widely to employers, consultants and invidivuals, so that many registers are no longer exclusive and duplication abounds. Many employers also believe that the rejects of other people's searches or advertisements must be good, so they try to avoid paying for an advertisement or an executive search themselves by pressing consultants to 'search their files'. This is both unpopular and unrewarding to the consultants; jobs and individuals are too specific and, as fees depend solely on appointment, so little effort is put into time-consuming and often fruitless searching (but see outplacement consultants below).

Selection consultants

Although all consultants offering recruitment services are termed 'recruitment consultants' – and often call themselves 'search consultants' quite wrongly – the selection consultant offers a very specific service. He or she is usually an experienced personnel or line manager and will handle a total recruitment assignment from initial advice through to presentation of a shortlist of suitable candidates. They differ from other consultants in that they use advertising – which the client pays for – as a means of attracting candidates. Some may add candidates from file, but this is unusual. Many also offer reduced services and will advise on any of the individual stages such as job analysis and specification; or drawing up, placing an advertisement and passing on replies unscreened. They may add some preliminary screening or help with the interviewing. Some are also able to offer psychological screening. Some will do this 'in house' at a daily rate, others will charge on an assignment basis. Apart from the expertise they have to offer, they are able to advertise over their own name and disguise that of their client, which many consider preferable to the use of a publication's box number.

Advertising agents

Some advertising agencies have set up their own recruitment consultancy service, usually on the lines of a selection consultancy. Others will offer only a reduced service such as all aspects of the advertising process plus, as required, the use of their own box number and initial screening of candidates (on paper). They may be able to offer interviewing facilities and the necessary administrative back-up. For a fuller description of the services of an advertising agency, see pages 33–4 above.

Outplacement consultants

These are a phenomenon of the last twenty years and reflect the fact that selection and executive search consultancies only act for employers and not for candidates (note that employment agencies do handle both and act more as an 'honest broker' – a subtle but important distinction often not understood by would-be candidates who bombard search and selection consultants with C.V.s, most of which are promptly destroyed). The outplacement consultancies arose in response to high levels of executive redundancy and initially offered counselling and sometimes psychologically based careers guidance and help with composing C.V.s. This extended to library services, secretarial help and finally marketing. Most worked initially for the individual, but as this is less profitable most now try to work exclusively for companies. Where they still work for individuals, these are usually high-calibre people who are seeking to make a career change but are not redundant. They maintain a register of current candidates from which they will make a selection; this is available, free of charge, to executive search and selection consultants as well as to employers.

Executive search consultants

This type of service was initially developed in the USA where, unlike in Europe, there were no established nationwide quality newspapers. US multinational companies then sought the same type of service in Europe and US executive search companies set up offices over here. Since then, although US influence is very strong, many independent executive search consultancies have been established in the UK and in most developed economies throughout the world. Their service is geared to top management and they act as private consultants to the board, often to the chief executive or the chairman. They offer a complete service: from detailed initial analysis of the need; drawing up of job descriptions and specifications; advice on the marketplace – availability of candidates, current salaries etc – identification, approach to and later assessment of candidates; presentation of one or more short-lists; detailed referencing; and finally help with the negotiation.

Executive search only works effectively where the number of possible candidates is relatively small, where they can be identified through their reputation and they are of sufficient maturity to handle the situation. In recent years, consultancies have arisen which offer only a partial service; where this is marketed as a true search, this can be very misleading. True executive search consultants usually belong to a professional association with a declared code of ethics.

The key difference from other services is that the executive search consultant identifies and approaches possible candidates individually after some considerable research – few if any will come from files – and the highest level of confidentiality is maintained; without this the service would not work. Most executive search consultants have themselves been top managers, which gives them a high personal credibility at the most senior levels. Their charges are high but, as there is no need to advertise, the total cost is comparable to that of selection consultants – and probably no higher than if recruitment was handled by the company's own top management.

Recruiting overseas

This can be done effectively in one of three ways:

Advertising
UK consultants
Overseas consultants

Advertising. All countries have a local press which is used regularly for recruitment purposes. Coverage and costs vary widely and there are local regulations and customs to consider. For example, in the former Western Germany there are two main newspapers, *Die Weldt* and the *FAZ*, each covering large geographical areas. One or both may be necessary (you may need also to use a third to cover southern Germany). Advertising is traditionally on a Saturday; as salaries may not be included, 'the size of the advertisement shows the importance of the job', so a larger space than necessary may have to be taken. In some countries foreign advertisements are taxed, so, in France for example, it pays to advertise in French with replies to a local box number. Although efforts are being made to develop EEC-wide newspapers (*The European*, for example), it will take time for these to become established. For British expatriates working abroad, the *Sunday Times* has traditionally been effective. However, fashions change and a good advertising agency can guide one through the jungle, provide samples and past experience, and ensure that your advertisement appears in the right place at the right time at the expected cost – no mean feat! If replies are received in another language, it is as well to know if there are any such language-speakers in the company; if not, translators are available – the agency may be able to help you.

UK consultants. Many are used to recruiting overseas, especially for the expatriate areas (the Middle East, Africa, the Far East). Many also have associates overseas with whom they work jointly. This is particularly useful if the market extends to several countries. Whether advertising or executive-search techniques are preferable will depend on the nature of the appointment and the scatter of candidates. Executive search gives great flexibility across a wide geographical spread (it is not uncommon in very high-tech appointments for the final shortlist to include candidates from, say, the USA, Germany and the UK). For multinational appointments there are advantages in the appointment being handled by someone from the parent country co-ordinating others overseas where necessary.

Overseas consultants. If the company has no overseas office (or no recruitment capability) and the need is for a local person, there are advantages in using an overseas consultancy for the depth of their understanding of the local people and practices as well as linguistic ability. A UK consultancy may make the introduction, or contact may be made direct. Strictly speaking, executive search is illegal in some countries and, although there are established ways of getting around this, it may be wiser to use a UK concern or to advertise. The calibre of international consultants is certainly as high, if not higher, as many in the UK!

Choosing a consultancy

Lists of consultancies appear regularly in such publications as *The Personnel Manager's Yearbook*, published by AP Information Services; *The Executive Grapevine*, published by the company of the same name, and many other recruitment guides (see Selected Bibliography starting on page 150).

The Federation of Recruitment and Employment Services (36–38 Mortimer Street, London W1N 7RB), the Institute of Management Consultants (32 Hatton Garden, London EC1), the Institute of Personnel Management (IPM House, Camp Road, Wimbledon, London SW19 4UX) and the Institute of Practitioners in Advertising (44 Belgrave Square, London SW1X 8QS) will all help an employer to find a suitable intermediary. The IPM issues a Code of Professional Conduct. A number of the larger executive-search concerns have published guidelines on selecting a consultancy (usually as a part of their own PR) and these can be obtained by writing to them direct. The following broad guidance applies to the selection of a consultancy:

Track record. Find out the history of the concern, what it was set up to do, how it has progressed, the type of work it typically handles and the extent of its organization/links.

Personnel. Find out about the track record of the principals: how well trained and experienced are they? What is their relevant experience and how recent is it? Who would handle the assignment and how suitable is his or her experience/training?

Modus operandi. Find out how they set about an assignment: preparatory work, documentation, progress reports, time scales, results and follow-up. What happens if things go wrong for whatever reason or if changes need to be made in mid-stream?

Fees. Find out how much they are going to charge and on what basis – a daily rate or a fee based on results. What is meant by 'expenses'? How are they calculated and invoiced?

References. Ask to talk to at least two recent clients and find out how satisfied they were with the services provided.

Reflections on recruitment

These *Reflections* focus attention on five different recruitment situations and illustrate some characteristic pitfalls. They emphasize the importance of looking at recruitment 'through the eyes of the candidate' and of anticipating the attitudes and reactions of prospective employees. Each *Reflection* depicts a separate situation, hence there is no need to read them in sequence. The various episodes, when considered as a whole, also show how general principles about recruitment in practice must be applied sensitively and sensibly to meet widely differing circumstances.

  I   The school leaver
 II   The factory operative
III   The computer programmer
 IV   The graduate
  V   The manager
 VI   The director

Author's Note The characters in these *Reflections* are wholly fictitious, they are unrelated to any people or companies with similar names. Alas, the events portrayed happen every day.

The school leaver

Local school leavers should be a firm's best source of supply of potential employees. To school leavers the act of starting work is a leap into the unknown. Their knowledge of the work available locally is derived largely from hearsay and much of that will seem dull and uninspiring. With improvements in the educational system, school leavers are becoming more discriminating when seeking their first job. Some employers fail to realize this as John Ashton was to discover:

'I'm John Ashton and I live in a council house in Wythenshawe. My dad's a fitter in an enginering firm at Trafford Park. My mum works part time in a school canteen. Ian, my brother, is an apprentice draughtsman and our Sally works in a shop. Sally and Bob, her husband, are living with us until she has a baby so they can get higher up the list for a council house.

'I go to Wythenshawe High School. I'm not in the top stream, but I'm doing OK. Next summer I'm taking GCSE and with a bit of luck should pass English, Maths, General Science and Technical Drawing. I don't know about the others. The school want me to stay on, but I'm fed up and want to earn some cash. I play football for one of the school teams and on Saturdays work at a local garage helping my mate Joe on the pumps, doing tyres and whatever. Last Christmas I bought an old bike with my savings and Joe is helping me to do it up.

'When I leave school I want to be a fitter like my dad. He says that if you've got a trade behind you, you'll never be out of work. Mind you, he's been made redundant a couple of times but seems to fall on his feet. I'd really like to be a draughtsman or a toolmaker: dad says that's where the money is, but you've got to learn the trade first. The careers teacher had us all in last week to find out what we want to do when we leave school. I told him and he said, "Get a good training. Join a firm with a good training scheme, like Supreme Engineering Company; you know, the one that showed us round their works just after Christmas. I wouldn't advise the Bricklands Machine Company, though. They won't let us take any of our pupils round and I reckon they must be ashamed of the place. Keep away from Dodgson's too. They call it an apprenticeship there, but they've no proper training school. Go and see Mrs Shingle, the youth employment officer, and pay attention to what she says." Mrs Shingle gave me some cards to take to several firms. This is what happened.

'The Clarefield Precision works isn't far off, so I went there first. At the main gate I was told to go to "the Employment" and I showed my card to a woman inside. She gave me a form and told me to fill it in. She also gave me a booklet to look at. I managed to fill in the form – it didn't want much and most of it like "previous jobs" didn't apply to me as I haven't done any. I waited about half an hour, then her 'phone buzzed and she took me in to see Mr Johnson, I think his name was.

'He had quite a nice office, though the chairs were a bit scruffy. He told me to sit down and started to read my form. After a few minutes (it seemed like hours) he said:

— So your name's John Ashton.
— Yes.
— And you live at – I can't read this – No 2 Hill Rise, Wythenshawe. Is that right?
— Yes.
— And you go to Wythenshawe High School.
— Yes.
— And you're taking GCSE this summer; how do you expect to get on?
— My teacher says he reckons I should get English, Maths, General Science, Technical Drawing and maybe one or two others.
— What do you think?
— I reckon that's about right.
— I see you list motor bike repairs as your main hobby.
— Well, I've got a bike – bought it at Christmas and Joe at the garage where I work on Saturdays . . .
— You work on Saturdays?
— Yes.
— Why didn't you say so before?
— I didn't think . . .
— Well you should. If you're going to be an apprentice, you've got to learn to think.
— Yes.
— Well, get on with it.
— Get on with what?
— Your bike, lad.
— Oh, Joe helped me hot it up a bit.
— Um – and now you tear up the estate at weekends, I suppose.
— *(No answer)*
— Why do you want to become an apprentice?
— Because my dad's a fitter and Tom, my brother, is a draughtsman and says it's all right and I want a trade behind me.
— Trade behind you?

— Yes – to fall back on.
— So you don't want to stay on the bench?
— No.
— Well, John, there's no point in going any further. We want lads who're prepared to work and work hard here. You take my advice and don't try to run before you can walk. Get a trade if you can, but don't go bothering about promotion at your age: if you're any good the firm'll look after you. Good morning.
— Good morning. Oh, do you want the card?
— Aye, I'll send it back to the youth employment officer.
— I see. I'll be off then. Good morning.

'My second card was for the Electrical and Mechanical Engineering Company. That didn't last long either. I had to go to the personnel department – all nicely set out like a doctor's surgery with books and flowers and things. I was told to make myself at home, after giving my name to the chap in uniform.

'When it was my turn, I went in. It was a nice comfortable-looking office and the woman – Mrs Whatever-it-was (I didn't catch her name) – seemed friendly. She shook hands and told me to sit down.

— Well, what can I do for you?
— I want an apprenticeship.
— What sort of apprenticeship?
— In engineering.
— Any particular trade?
— A fitter or something like that.
— Do you know anything about fitting, what it involves, the different types and so on?
— My dad's a fitter – so I think I do.
— Good. How well are you doing at school?
— I'm taking GCSE this summer and reckon I'll get English, Maths, Technical Drawing and General Science.
— And how well do you think you will get on?
— My teacher says I should pass with a bit of luck.
— Where do you usually come in class?
— About average except in Technical Drawing, where I was

top last term, and I usually do quite well in Maths and Science; they're my favourite subjects.

— Fine. Well now, I'm going to give you a form to fill in and a booklet telling you all about us and our training scheme. Then I want you to come back on Tuesday next week and sit some tests. Have you any questions you'd like to ask me?

— How much do I get?

— I can't remember exactly, but it's all in the booklet.

— Do I have to take these tests?

— Yes.

— I haven't any more questions.

— All right then. Let the commissionaire have your form when you've filled it in and we'll see you on Tuesday at 8.30 am.

'I went outside to the waiting room and had a quick look at the form – there were eight pages of it asking questions about my dad, my mum, whether they were married, divorced and so on. A bit of cheek, I thought – and it would take me hours to complete it. I told the bloke I'd take it home and bring it in tomorrow.

'I looked at my other cards. I decided to go next to the Supreme Engineering Company. I went to the main gate and one of the chaps showed me where the personnel department was. They took my card and told me to sit down and wait a minute. It was a nice room, clean and tidy with pictures on the walls. Photographs of some of the things they make there – looked quite good too. The secretary said:

— Mr Smith will see you now. Would you like to leave your coat here?

'I went in. Mr Smith was the chap who showed us round before – leastways he was in charge – apprentices actually took us round, and he'd given us a talk: quite interesting it was. He got up, shook hands and asked me what I wanted to do after I'd left school. He talked in a friendly way about the training scheme, what I would do and so on. Then he said:

— I'd like you to let us have some information about yourself on this form and then come back for another interview next week. What we do is give you some tests and then a couple of us will have a chat with you. We do this for all people like yourself. The tests tell us if you have any special abilities that you haven't had a chance to develop at school. This helps us to see whether you would make a good fitter – or a better machinist – or perhaps might become a draughtsman or something like that. They're specially designed for people like yourself, and I don't think you'll find them too bad at all. And then we have another talk with you to find out just what you really want to do and give you a chance to ask us any questions you like. Now is there anything you would like to ask me at this stage?

– Well, no, I think you've told me all I want to know at the moment. Thank you very much.

'When I was outside I glanced at the form he'd given me. It didn't look too bad – but there would be tests again. Still, they didn't sound too bad from the way he'd explained them. Perhaps I've got some hidden talent! Not likely – but it's worth a try. I'll fill this one in tonight and see what happens before I go trailing around any more places. But I suppose I'd better see what dad's got to say first.'

Commentary

School leavers, especially those of above average ability, are perceptive and sensitive when they visit a succession of different firms. John's reactions illustrate some practical points which are often overlooked. His reception and the attitudes of the people he meets tell him a lot about the firm. They reveal something of the social framework within which he might shortly be asked to work. His first impressions stick fast and colour everything else. John will respond to a reasonable challenge inside a known framework, but will fight shy of the unknown. His reaction to tests is fairly common. The subject always needs to be introduced carefully even at a preliminary meeting, as well as when the tests are later being administered. It is important to recognize that the interviewer needs a deep understanding of the adolescent's world. Initial communication and rapport are difficult to establish. The interviewer belongs to the 'they' group, the authoritarian adult world mistrusted by so many young people. Understanding and insight will help the interviewer to make a realistic appraisal of John through sensitive questioning and probing of attitudes. It is necessary to guard against the danger of interpreting too superficially the dogmatic utterances which many youngsters are prone to blurt out. The successful recruitment of school leavers requires a long term plan. The well-informed personnel officer will realize that most school leavers take their parents' advice, with careers teachers and youth employment officers supplying information and acting as liaison officers. (Proper vocational guidance is virtually impossible when the youth employment officer can allow only ten minutes per applicant.) Time invested by a firm in ensuring that it merits a good local reputation as an employer repays ample dividends. This can be assisted by regular contacts with careers teachers and youth employment officers; taking part in local careers conventions; talks to schools; inviting school parties to tour the factory; and by making information available through the local newspapers. Even more important, the youngsters already employed will influence the attitudes of others in the district. It is easy enough to agree with these abstract propositions, but if John Ashton applied to your firm today, what would be his reactions?

(i) Would he already have heard favourable comments from relations, friends, careers teacher and youth employment officer?
(ii) Would he receive an encouraging reception?
(iii) Would you have a suitable application form?
(iv) Would your recruitment literature mean anything to him?
(v) Would he be seen by a trained interviewer chosen for his or her understanding of school leavers and skill in assessment?
(vi) Would he go away feeling that he was wanted and would be fairly assessed?

The factory operative

The major part of the recruitment activity in many companies consists of finding and engaging factory operatives and other shop floor employees. During periods of expansion or high labour turn-over, this work is going on all the time. In spite of this, or perhaps because of it, recruitment arrangements sometimes allow the most alarming things to happen. This is so particularly if inadequately trained staff are exposed to severe pressure of work. A casual or disorganized approach proves very costly in the long run. On reading the exploits of Millie Scattergood, most personnel officers will indignantly protest 'It couldn't happen here.' They may well be right; but some weaknesses creep into even the most efficient employment departments from time to time.

Ms Pritchard was very busy. It was Monday morning and she had a waiting room full of applicants. For payroll vacancies she did not use application forms, nor had she troubled to look up her records of previous employees. Otherwise, she would have seen one card dated 3 9 '85 and signed J G Chance. It read 'Millie Scattergood should not be re-employed without reference to me'. Mr Chance was a foreman then, now he was works manager. Millie's reappearance had been prompted by an advertisement in the local paper.

WHY NOT COME OUT TO WORK AGAIN?

In 5 weeks you could earn enough to buy a new cooker. In 10 weeks enough to buy an automatic washer. In 20 weeks enough for a holiday in the Bahamas!
Come and see us and learn something to your advantage.

Call and see Ms G Pritchard,
Personnel Officer

WRAP-IT-UP QUICKLY COMPANY
Rugby

Ms Pritchard sighed and pressed her buzzer. Millie walked in. She sat down as close to Ms Pritchard as possible, so that she could see anything that was written down.

— Good morning Miss . . . er . . . Mrs . . . ?
— Mrs Scattergood.
— Mrs Scattergood?
— Yes. I've come for a job. Harry Jackson said he'd give me one in his department.
— Well, Mrs Scattergood, I don't think we've any vacancies in that department. But we do . . .
— Oh, yes you have. Harry told me that one of his girls is being moved to another machine and I could have her job. I saw him on Saturday night in the King's Arms.
— Did he? It's the first I've heard of it, but I'll have a word with him in a few minutes. Now, what experience . . .

The telephone rang and she broke off to answer it.

— Yes, Harry. She's with me now.

Ms Pritchard tried desperately to wave Millie outside, but Millie pretended not to understand and remained glued to her seat.

— Well, Harry, you might have told me before. She tells me you promised her a job on Saturday. I think you'd better see her and explain the position. I'll send her up now. Experience? Oh yes I think so. (Millie nodded as if to say 'I know all there is to know about injection moulding.')

A confused Ms Pritchard replaced the telephone.

— Well, Mrs Scattergood, if you'll wait outside a moment I'll arrange for someone to take you up to the department.
— What's it worth?
— I beg your pardon?
— What's the rate for the job?
— How do I know. I don't even know what the *job* is. You'd better ask Mr Jackson.

Ten minutes later the office junior took Millie up to the department. The interview with Harry was brief; brief and painful for Harry; brief and rewarding for Millie.

— Hallo, Harry.

— Hallo, Millie. Hang on a minute while I just finish this.

— All right. Oh, there's our Rosie. Is it all right if I say hallo to her while I'm waiting?

— Yes, I suppose so.

Millie tripped across to Rosie.

— Here, Rosie, what's the job like that young Sheila Smith's doing? Harry says she'll be moving and I can have it.

— She seems to sit there and just twiddle a few knobs. There doesn't seem much to it, as far as I can see.

— Is it hot?

— No, not really. No hotter than the oven!

— Sitting down, isn't it?

— Yes, all the time.

— Near you?

— Yes. Leastways if I shift myself along the bench a bit . . . What's the rate?

— I don't know yet – I'll have to ask Harry.

— Didn't Pritchard tell you?

— She didn't know anything about it.

— That's even better: tell Harry it's £3.50; so far, Harry's only had a girl on it at £3.10. Tell him that's what you thought Pritchard said. If he swallows it, we'll have some fun.

— Right. I'd better go. Harry's waiting for me.

— Sorry Harry. Well, now about this job. Reckon I could do it with my hands tied behind my back.

— Ever done it before?

— Well, not exactly. But from what I can see, it's no more difficult than cooking Bert's lunch. I've done similar jobs, you know.

— Oh. The trouble is, Millie, that I haven't definitely arranged to move young Sheila yet: it's going to be difficult.

— Yes, but you can manage that Harry, if I know you. My Bert says it's good for the youngsters to move around a bit.

— Yes, I dare say he does. Well, I'll have a word with Mr Chance.

— Mr Chance? Can't you run your own department without him putting his big nose in?

- Yes, of course . . . All right, Millie. I'll see what I can do.
- Does that mean I can start?
- Just give me half an hour to think about it. You go back to personnel and I'll give them a ring.
- Sounds like you're trying to get out of it to me.
- No, that's not it.
- Then why not say so now?
- Look here, Millie . . . Oh all right, you can have the job. I'll tell personnel.
- I understand the rate's £3.50.
- Who told you that? Sounds a bit high to me.
- That's what Ms Pritchard said.
- Oh well, she should know. We'll pay you £3.50 plus piece work with 100 per cent guaranteed during the first fortnight's learning time.
- That's great, Harry. I'll just go down to personnel and sign myself in. 'Bye for now.

Commentary

There are probably very few personnel departments as badly organized as this one. On the other hand, there are quite a number where this sort of thing is liable to happen during temporary absences or when the personnel officer is very busy. Millie, of course, was pretty shrewd and knew how to turn things to her advantage. But she is not unique: most firms encounter their Millies from time to time. Why did she get away with it? Let us consider a few of the major errors.

The advertisement was woolly. It said nothing about the jobs available nor about the terms of employment. Perhaps these had not been really thought out: later events certainly suggest this. Before any advertisement is published, the personnel officer should have a clear idea – preferably in writing – of the jobs to be filled and the sort of people needed, together with rates of pay and other employment conditions. If Ms Pritchard had done her homework Millie might never have applied but, even if she had, the interview would have been easier to control. Millie had the advantage throughout and the interview was a farce. She was a difficult person to deal with but Ms Pritchard was courting disaster. Contrary to her belief, application forms for factory employees are not a waste of time. An application form could have told her a great deal about Millie. And if the personnel department had been better organized, Millie's record of previous employment with the firm would have come to light, and Mr Chance would have been consulted in time. The interview room was badly arranged with Millie sitting so close to Ms Pritchard that she could read notes and overhear her telephone conversation. The latter was disastrous in more ways than one. Any interruption destroys an important feature of an interview – rapport between the parties – and disturbs the flow of information. In this particular case, Ms Pritchard could have firmly insisted that Millie left the room; alternatively, she could have taken the call in the next office if her secretary had been filtering incoming telephone calls.

It is probably tactful to draw a veil over the 'interviews' as such. They neither sought, obtained, nor gave information according to any systematic plan. Ms Pritchard failed to make an effective assessment of Millie, which it was her responsibility to do whether Harry was offering her a job or not. Harry's interview performance was no better. It would be unfair to blame him for being unaware of Mr Chance's note, as Ms Pritchard let him down badly in that respect. To be charitable, we can assume that Harry's firm had overlooked that he was untrained in recruitment. Even some elementary training in employment interviewing would have directed his attention to Millie's lack of experience and to the reasons why she had left her previous jobs. He would have found compelling grounds for withdrawing his rash statement of the previous Saturday – even though Millie was well-known to him socially. Instead he allowed his embarrassment to override his common sense. The wage situation as it developed became an intriguing one! It is always prudent to look up wage rates carefully, as Harry and Ms Pritchard will undoubtedly discover to their cost.

If Millie turns up at your firm when you are taking your well-earned holiday, what exactly will happen? Will there be:

  (i) woolly advertisements which invite her presence?
 (ii) an inadequately staffed personnel department and a distraught, disorganized recruitment officer?
(iii) an interview situation which she can exploit to her advantage?
 (iv) no provision for application forms to be completed?

(v) a foreman as inept and untrained as Harry?

The computer programmer

Many women suffer from discrimination at some stage in their career 'in a man's world'. If you have also been born into an ethnic minority, bias and prejudice against you are even more likely. If you fight back, you are labelled 'an aggressive feminist'. Most employers would deny that they discriminate unfairly or that they are biased or prejudiced. Chrissie felt otherwise . . .

Christine – she called herself Chrissie – was brought up in Surbiton. At the age of six months her West African parents had fostered her out to an English nanny – a kindly middle-aged spinster. Chrissie stayed behind when her parents returned to Africa in order to have an English education. When her mother died, Chrissie was adopted and changed her name from Abolengo to Johnstone, after her foster mother. Educated privately, Chrissie made few friends, as most were reluctant to invite her home. There were exceptions, of coure, but Chrissie learned early the art of hiding her feelings and 'keeping a low profile'. Academically she found it hard to concentrate and just scraped five O Levels, including Maths and English. When she left school, teachers and her foster mother pushed hard and got her into a major high street bank which promised her training and a career. She tried hard, passed her early training and exams and learned the routines of banking – though without enthusiasm. She found it too restrictive and disliked the uniform, which did not suit her colouring or personality. Customers at the counter often showed hostility, which made her nervous; when she made a minor error, they sometimes made a lot of fuss and demanded to see the manager. Chrissie decided to leave.

Her next job didn't last long either. The travel agency was more fun and she started to learn how to use a computer, but she found working all day in artificial light tiring and felt she was getting nowhere – though she enjoyed the lonely free weekend in Amsterdam. She started a secretarial course and achieved average grades, but trying to get a job was a nightmare. She would be called for interview, but then . . .

— Christine Johnstone is here to see you, sir. (Did she detect a meaningful look?)
— Send her in. (Pause.)
— Oh hello, Miss Johnstone. Please sit down.
(There was a disconcerting pause, after which they discussed briefly her school and work record.)
— You've moved around a lot?
— I felt I was not getting anywhere.
— Ever thought of returning to Africa?
— I've never been there, so I can't return!
— Quite. Do you think you could fit in here?
— I don't see why not.
— No – er – no. Most do; we're a happy, friendly crowd, you know.

Chrissie didn't know, or did she . . . ?

— Well thank you very much for coming, there are several other candidates to see. We'll let you know.
— Is that all?
— Yes, that's all for the moment. Janice will show you out.

He rang his bell . . . Nothing to put her finger on, but Chrissie felt she knew she was not wanted.

Her next job seemed promising. Chrissie was given some training in word processing – WordStar – and her curiosity was aroused. She started to talk to the programmers. Charlie was friendly and helpful. They had a drink after work on Fridays and Chrissie invited him home. Miss Johnstone made him welcome, a little uncomfortably so, but Charlie was good-natured and Chrissie thrilled. Charlie promised to help her to learn more about computer programming and invited her to his flat. It soon transpired that there was a price to pay. Chrissie was prepared for it but, having deep religious convictions, did not want a casual affair. Charlie made promises. Chrissie gave way – and felt dirty and used. Charlie's triumph went round the office and she became the butt of nods, winks and touches. She tried to ignore it but eventually could take no more. She tried to talk to her supervisor but, as she had a 'reputation' and was openly living with one of the young graduates, Chrissie was told to forget it and be glad that the boys liked her; not all coloured girls were popular. If she didn't like it . . . Chrissie did not like it, and felt angry. Should she claim sexual harassment and take her employers to court or something? She spoke to a solicitor friend, but when it became clear that she would have to give evidence to a tribunal Chrissie quickly backed off.

She 'signed on' and was told about a government training scheme in computer programming. She decided to take it and had to sit an aptitude test battery first. She found that she had done well.

— You're full of surprises, Chrissie – you're really bright, you know. You should have gone to university. The scores suggest that you would have done well.

Chrissie was surprised and delighted and tackled the course with enthusiasm. She did well, fell in love with a fellow student and, after much soul-searching, decided that the time had come for her to leave home and moved into his London flat.

The agency which specialized in computer vacancies was very confident and made some appointments for her. The first – a computer services bureau – had two major clients and many smaller ones. She would join the programming team and later handle some accounts of her own. Full of confidence, she dressed to suit herself, preferring strong colours, large earrings and fashionable clothes. She was no longer ashamed of her African background. Her experiences had also made her more aggressive.

— Come in, come in, Chrissie, you do look smart. Mind if I call you Chrissie?
— Suits me.
— Well, Chrissie, I've had an excellent report about you; seems you created quite an impression on the course. You've moved around a bit, but we don't mind about that as you have built up some useful experience.

He smiled; Chrissie smiled back guardedly.

— How do you feel about the work we do here?
— Sounds interesting. How long would it be before I could deal with clients?
— Oh, that will take a little time, Chrissie – you've got to learn the ropes first.
— Yes, I understand; but how long will it be – months or years?
— It will depend on you and on the client's business.
— Is there a problem with me being black and a woman?

He looked embarrassed.

— They're irrelevant in today's world, aren't they?
— Are they?
— Well it depends on the client, I suppose. Some prefer to deal with a man; some don't mind and race doesn't come into it – provided you can speak good, clear English; it depends on the expertise needed and the ability to communicate, especially with lay-people. Some do have difficulty in accepting an – er – aggressive woman or those with a really thick accent, but I don't think that would apply in your case. At the end of the day it's the client who calls the shots.

This took some digesting. Of course it was true, but no-one had ever put these things into words before. Should she give him credit for honesty or scorn his commercial pragmatism? Chrissie said she would let them know, as she had arranged to see several other firms (she marvelled at her own cheek; but that's what they usually say to me, she said to herself defiantly). It was taken with equanimity. They too had other candidates to see but stressed that they would like to consider her further if she could confirm her interest.

Three others told a similar story, though not quite so openly. She found herself in demand, which boosted her ego and gave her the chance to concentrate on the strength of the business and the kind of people who worked there. The service business was commercially vulnerable, especially in a time of recession, and she didn't want the trauma of redundancy; on the other hand, large companies were also vulnerable and progress was painfully slow. She had enterprise and wanted to be able to find an outlet for it.

She discussed her feelings with the computer recruitment agency and finally settled for the first company she had seen. They had helped her to put things in their true perspective. They were honest and she liked the kind of person who worked there. She knew she was good and prepared to work hard. Maybe she could find some clients who would demand she handled their affairs – after all, she might set up on her own one day . . .

Commentary

If Chrissie applied for a vacancy in your company how would she be received? Try this checklist:

1 Would she be treated with courtesy by all she met – security staff, receptionist, your secretary, yourself?
2 Would she detect bias, prejudice or discrimination of any kind in the questions she was asked, in response to her questions or in the tests she was given?
3 Would she be told honestly about the scope for promotion?
4 How would you deal with the case of sexual harassment?

Or are all of these things covered by bland policy statements whose application is not seriously monitored or abuses checked?

The graduate

Graduate recruitment is a perennial nightmare in many companies. It can also be costly and very time-consuming. Employers, students and university appointments boards are all conscious that they have some mutual interests, but find it uncommonly difficult to tune in to the same wavelength. Fewer mistakes would be made if employers accepted the proposition that graduates are likely to be perceptive as well as intelligent. They will probably go to some trouble to find out their own market value and to make diligent enquiries about any company which invites them to join its ranks. Their attitudes will be conditioned by what they see when visiting a firm as well as by what they read from the firm's handouts and brochures. Undergraduates talk amongst themselves about career prospects and each common room has its equivalent of a consumers' guide which, although unwritten, sets out to answer the question *which employer?* At times 'good' undergraduates can count on receiving two offers for every three applications they make, there is more than a suspicion that it is they who choose the employer rather than the other way round. Charles Newton was able to do this – and he is certainly not alone in that respect.

Charles Newton's father had no doubt that his son was 'a chip off the old block' and should make his career in export sales. Charles was inclined to agree. His father, a director of British Exporters Ltd, had fixed him up with vacation jobs which had given him a chance to see something of export sales activities in several different companies. In this respect, Newton had the edge on most of his contemporaries at his university. Their vacations had been spent travelling or doing mundane clerical and manual jobs. They had found the cash useful – but the experience had put them off industry for life. Newton saw in export sales an opportunity to use his knowledge of modern languages, in which his tutor had said that he should get a second. He also reckoned that he would find individual responsibility, personal freedom and good prospects of promotion. Now in his final year at university, he availed himself of a talk with the assistant secretary of the appointments board. Newton wanted to confirm his own impressions and to be put in touch with the right sort of companies. Having looked down a long list of firms who said they wanted arts graduates, Newton eliminated some of them on the spot. The common room gossip had forwarned him that these were unattractive. The discussion produced a shortlist of four firms which sounded interesting. Newton duly glanced at their brochures (some were out of date) and rummaged among the file copies of company reports. Browsing again through *The Directory of Opportunities for Graduates*, his eye was struck by International Electricals Ltd. He added its name to his shopping list. On Newton's behalf, the assistant secretary wrote to the personnel manager of all five companies and he was duly invited to meet the company's representatives. As the appointments board had only limited interviewing accommodation to offer, several companies suggested meeting for a preliminary discussion at a hotel in January 'when our university recruiting team will be visiting your area'. Newton consulted the common room for guidance on protocol.

— *You'll have to wear your dark lounge suit, college tie and polish your shoes – and get your hair cut. Be as conventional as you can. Don't forget to have some questions ready to ask them.*
— *Questions?*
— *Anything they like talking about. Their overseas trade position, their training scheme, what they would expect you to be doing in five years' time: that sort of thing. Careful about salaries: leave that until last, then raise it in a casual way – they like that. Tell them how hard you have worked (not too hard mind, or they will think you are dim) and how you struck a good balance between work and pleasure. You have benefited as widely as possible from university life and like meeting people from other countries – but for heaven's sake tone down the parties and boozing side. Good luck. Don't let them talk you into making a decision on the spot. Go and have a look at the place before committing yourself, and make sure the salary is in writing before you accept the job.*

Heeding these words of worldly wisdom, Newton duly presented himself for the preliminary interviews. There was little to choose between them. A typical one ran rather like this. It lasted about 20 minutes and there were two interviewers.

— Ah, come in, come in. You must be – let me see now – Charles Percival Strang-Newton.
(Newton winced. Why had his parents strung his name out like that. Didn't sound right in the industrial context).
— Yes, that's right.
— Good, good. Sit down won't you.
(Casual eyes watched his every movement).
— Well now. My name is Arkwright – not the inventor of the engine, you know – ha, ha. And this is my colleague, Sally Anderson. She is assistant chief technical officer in charge of all apprentice training and recruitment. I'm from personnel.
— How do you do.

- How do you do. Now then, could you tell us all about yourself?
- Well – er yes, but what do you want to know?
- What you have done in life so far – your home, schools, exams, what you're doing here and so on.
(Newton outlined his career to date.)
- Good, good. Are you expecting to get a good degree?
- My tutor says I should get an upper second.
- Good, and what do you think?
- I hope she's right.
- Ha, ha. And so do we! so do we!
- About how long do you work daily?
- About average, I suppose.
- Good. And what do you think you have got out of your time here – other than a degree?
- I've had a chance to meet all sorts of people.
- *All* sorts of people?
- Yes, you know, people from all over the world.
- That's fine, fine. Now what do you want to do when you graduate?
- I had thought about export sales.
- Any particular product?
- No, not really.
- You would have to learn all about it of course.
- Of course.
- You wouldn't mind that?
- I should like to.
- That's fine, fine.
Any questions, Sally?
- No, I don't think so.
- Well now, Mr – er – Strang-Newton, have you any questions you'd like to ask us?
- Yes, one or two if I may. What is your export trading position?
- I'm glad you asked that question.
(Mr Arkwright expanded on this at length.)
- Any other questions?
- Yes, could you please tell me a little about your training scheme?
(Ms Anderson did so at length.)

– One final question: could you give me a general idea of what my salary progression would be likely to be?
– Ah, yes, salary. (Long pause while he ferreted among some papers.)
– Yes, salary – here we are. Arts graduate, second class honours: starting salary – £8,500. That's about the market rate, isn't it? (It *was* two years ago, Newton thought, remembering the common room discussion.)
– Just a nominal one you know, while you're under training. And after that – well, it's up to you.
– I see. What might I be earning by the time I am 30?
– Oh, that's very hard to say. Depends on how you progress. But we aim to keep all salaries under review and you'll have to leave that to us. Isn't that right, Sally?
– Yes, that's right.
– Any more questions? (He looked at his watch rather obviously.)
– I don't think so.
– Good. Well the next stage will be for you to come and see us during your Easter vacation, when we can have a better look at you and we'll see where we go from there. Will you be free on 14 April?
– (Newton consulted his diary.) Yes.
– Good. Well we'll write to confirm it. Oh, and perhaps you would fill in this application form and send it on to us in the meantime. Good morning.
– Good morning.

'All running to form' (he later reported to his friends). Seems I shall be busy during the Easter vac!

At Easter Newton went the rounds. The procedure varied a bit, some companies making a bit of a splash (a room at the best hotel: lunch in the board room, taxi to the station, first class rail fare. 'Rather pleasant but quite unnecessary', thought Newton. 'Bet they're making a good profit.') Others gave him a glimpse of later reality (accommodation at local boarding house where other trainees were staying, and lunch in the canteen). 'A bit

Spartan', he thought. 'Don't take much trouble over their recruitment – canteen's as bad as the refectory. Still, I know what I'd
be letting myself in for: with a vengeance.')

He also went to a couple of recruitment fairs, one at the Exhibition Centre in Birmingham and the other in Lyons, France. He
found these a bit overwhelming at first but gradually found his
way round and learned the art of doing a quick circuit before
committing himself to a stall. At the end of the day he was
weighed down with brochures and leaflets and made many promises which he doubted he would have time to keep. The fair in
Lyons was fascinating. He stayed with an old school friend, Maurice, and together they surveyed the great exhibition. 'My friend,
you must endeavour to speak French; it will be very good practice
for you. Come, I will tell you what I know about the companies
as we go round. In France you will get a very thorough training
and in Germany also. It will be a very good start for you for a
career in export sales, *n'est-ce pas?*' Charles agreed, did the rounds
trying to use his French (they all tried to talk to him in English!)
and arranged to follow several opportunities up.

The selection procedures varied from another and longer interview with the recruiting officer plus a chat with one of the managers, to a two-day affair with tests and group discussion as well
as the inevitable interviews. He told his friends about it later.

— *We were herded together in a waiting room and introduced
to the others. After a while a character came in, told us what
we had let ourselves in for and sorted out our expenses – no
chance of making anything there!! Then they gave us some
intelligence tests – none of them said why. I should have
thought that a degree was sufficient indication, anyway. After
that, we had coffee with the interviewing panel – interesting
to see how they reacted to each other. One chap was even
running down his own company in our hearing: that one was
out! The next torture rack was the discussion group. We all
sat in a circle pretending to be nice and friendly, and they
gave us some inane subjects to discuss. 'What factors should
be taken into consideration when choosing where to go for a
holiday?' was one: couldn't be bothered with that. And
another 'Is privatization of all major industries inevitable?' I
ask you, at a nationalized industry! We all willingly gave the*

acceptable answers. Another was something about analyzing our reasons for failing to export enough and saying how we might do something about it. Quite interesting that one, but had to be cautious – thought they bristled a bit when I said trading on a good name was out. Don't think I'd go there. Don't know what they reckon they learned about us – how much we knew about the subject, I suppose – must ask one of the psychology students some day.

Then we had the interviews. Usually longish affairs going over every detail of your life. Most of them don't so much as ask a by your leave, before they want to know whether your father still lives with your mother. Damned cheek. One woman handled it very well though – can't think why the others didn't do the same. She said something like 'I've had a good look at your application form and the notes I made when we met at the Salisbury Hotel, so I don't want to go over that ground again.' (Wish the rest had bothered to do so: one chap asked me which university I was at and it was staring him in the face!) She went on: 'Now I want to get to know a bit about you as a person, the things you're really looking for in life, how far you're hoping to go, what is going to be important to you when choosing your job. The more you can tell me, the better I shall be able to see whether we have the right job for you. Take your time: I've set aside about three-quarters of an hour for our chat.' I liked that – told her a bit more than I should have, I expect, but she seemed really interested and, well, I suppose the more they know about you the better they can fix you up.

The ones that really got me down were those who obviously had no idea what they were going to do with you. Take International Electricals Ltd. So far as I could see, they want arts graduates because their engineers can't speak foreign languages, but they haven't a clue what to do with them when they've got them. Waffled vaguely about seeing something of manufacture and home sales before going on the export side in about five years' time – and had no idea how she was going to train me. We'll sort that out when you get here – depending on your progress' – called it 'a flexible training scheme'. If you ask me, it was an excuse and I doubt if they've ever had an arts graduate before. Won't entrust them

*with my future, I can tell you. Would you? By contrast, take
the computer firm and the oil company I saw: no vagueness
there, I'm not saying that I liked – or agreed with – all their
ideas, but at least they've been training graduates for years
and could give a straight answer to your questions.*

*I decided on Oil International finally: knew what they were
doing and where they were going. Took some trouble over
their recruitment and employed people in the personnel
department who knew their job and interviewed you properly.
Salary's good too – not outstanding – but fair, and prospects
are good. Met someone there who was here three or four
years ago; nice chap – doing quite well, too. Think I could
fit in there and make the most of myself. Better see about
getting a decent degree now, I suppose.*

Commentary

Few graduates have any detailed knowledge of industry or of the
choices open to them. They realize that they still have a lot to
learn and, on the whole, look to their first employer to provide
it. Within reason they are prepared to accept a company's claims
for its training arrangements. But a graduate is likely to become
suspicious if a company fails to explain in simple language why it
wants graduates and what it intends doing with them now and in
the future. Their suspicions are often justified. A common danger
signal is the bland claim 'our training arrangements are designed
to meet the particular requirements of each individual'. It is far
more convincing to produce one or two sample training programmes or to outline the career patterns of several previous
trainees. And if the company has a satisfied graduate trainee, why
not get him or her to help with the recruitment programme? Their
reports may be worth hearing too!

The selection procedures must be appropriate and they must
be explained. Intelligence tests will reveal more than 'enough
ability to obtain a degree', if they are administered and interpreted
by a trained person – so why not say so? Group procedures, too,
need explanation before they are inflicted on a bunch of people
who are not in a position to protest. The preliminary interview
does little more than give each party a chance to form a general
impression of the other. The fuller interview which comes later

should be prefaced by an explanation of its purpose. The interviewer should ensure that the graduate knows what is expected and is motivated to respond fully. Otherwise, the interview can be fraught with misunderstanding. A graduate usually lives a full life and is liable to hold forth on subjects which the interviewer does not wish to pursue, unless given firm guidance from an interviewer who is familiar with the undergraduate way of life.

Until recently, the role of many appointments boards has been mainly that of liaison between the faculty, student and the prospective employer. The better informed a board is about a company, the more likely is it that the board will be able to help. The usual glossy brochure is less informative than would be the career patterns of one or two successful graduate trainees. The influence of faculty staff should not be underestimated, particularly in the scientific and technological fields. Some students rely wholly on their advice – and personal contacts – instead of registering with the appointments boards. They would not be human if they did not steer their protégés towards companies which they know from their personal knowledge to have significant research or design facilities and to have scientific aims akin to their own.

There is some substance in the criticism that companies do not always know why they are recruiting graduates or what they are going to do with them once they have got them. This may be apparent to the graduates, even at the preliminary interview stage; and it is better that they should find out during the selection process, rather than discover it after they have been with the company for three months. At least they will be spared the frustration which comes from boredom, even though the prospective employers are frustrated in their short term and short sighted recruitment aims. The appointments boards have the unenviable task of acting as honest broker between two parties who may not have defined clearly what they have to offer, and who find it hard to communicate with each other. Research studies suggest that the typical graduate would like her/his first job to be one which:

(a) enables her to make direct use of her degree knowledge;
(b) offers opportunities for early responsibility and freedom of action;
(c) enables him to prove himself by making a recognizable contribution to the enterprise;

(d) keeps open the possibility of moving to different work, partly to broaden her experience, and partly as insurance in case her own interests should change after exposure to an environment which is at present unknown to her.

These aspirations do not seem unreasonable, nor are they incompatible with the reasons given by companies for recruiting graduates. These often include, with varying emphasis: the intake of potential managers from whose ranks the company's future leaders are expected to emerge; the topping up of the professional sector of its labour force; and the acquisition of a few of the more able people of each generation, in order that the company will be equipped to keep pace with new developments in the future. Not all graduates can rise to the top in industry; not all of them have the talent and ambition to do so. The post war years saw many mistakes in recruitment through excessive zeal on the part of employers and reliance on the naïve assumption that a university degree was itself a passport to success in industry. Both employers and graduates have become somewhat disenchanted as a result. In the national interest, it is worth going to a good deal of trouble to ensure that graduates are constructively engaged in tasks which they can do well. The country can ill-afford to have some of its best brains misapplied or underemployed.

Let us go back for a moment to Charles Newton and assume that he is due to be interviewed by your company tomorrow:

(i) Are you sure that the work demands a university education or could it be performed satisfactorily by a young person with appropriate A levels and three years' practical experience?

(ii) Have you planned how you will train the graduate and keep him/her constructively employed?

(iii) Would she/he have a predictable avenue of promotion or might he/she become frustrated and leave?

(iv) What proportion of the graduates recruited by your company have left within three years of engagement? Within five years?

(v) Would Charles Newton be convinced by your answers to these questions?

(vi) Would he be right to be convinced?

The manager

Personnel managers do not often recruit and select other personnel managers. Paradoxical as it may seem, that is one reason for asking Joan Beresford, who is 'one of us', to describe how she changed her job. She found herself for a little while on the other side of the interviewer's desk. The typical reader of this publication will only do so three or four times during the whole of his or her working life. Perhaps that explains why so many mistakes are made when conducting recruitment and selection work for managerial appointments. At this level, it is particularly necessary to anticipate what the would-be-candidate will be looking for – and to plan every step of the recruitment campaign with this in mind. It is worth considering what we ourselves might regard as important when changing jobs; and to contemplate what our reactions, as candidates, might be to the recruitment activities of our own firm. Some lessons can be learnt which have general relevance to the filling of other managerial positions.

21 October 1990

Dear Jack,

Many thanks for acting as one of my referees. I've accepted the job, and shall be starting there next month. Hope you didn't have to perjure yourself too much – I'll buy you a large whisky next time we meet! Sorry I wasn't able to go into details on the telephone, but I'm very pleased with the way things finally turned out. I thought you might be amused to know the background, so I'm enclosing some of the 'documents in the case'. Let me have them back eventually – I should love to have your comments.

I had been thinking of making a move for some time, but I didn't want the word to get around. In many ways I have been very happy here, but gradually became bored with running a department which somebody else had set up in a firm which is thoroughly sold on the value of good personnel management. Of course, some people would say I'm crazy to move! But I want a job with some challenge in it, a chance to build up something from scratch and to try out some of my own ideas.

I read a good many advertisements before I found anything that sounded suitable. Really, some of those advertisements!

They tell you virtually nothing about the company or the size of the job. As for salary – conspicuous by its absence in most cases. I must say, it made me take a new look at our own advertisements; it's salutary to see things from the other side of the fence occasionally. Well, to cut a long story short, two jobs caught my eye – one advertised by a firm of consultants and the other was in a personnel magazine. They appeared at about the same time and I decided to have a go at both.

The consultants asked me to meet their Mr Connell who was handling the assignment. He briefed me on the company, giving me a chance to get the feel of the total job situation, including possible snags. He'd obviously studied my application form pretty carefully, because he soon got down to business. Incidentally, have you seen one of their application forms? It concentrates on the important things, with a final section which is a sort of autobiography, self-analysis and the opportunity to sell yourself. It takes some filling in, but gives you a chance to do yourself justice – and presumably helps them with their initial sifting.

The interview lasted 1¼ hours so he had plenty of time to get to the bottom of things and give me a chance to ask questions. I wish I had time to interview in depth like that. Going home on the train, I jotted down what I could remember of one part and I'm enclosing it with this letter in case you're interested.

Well, he put me on the short list and I agreed to let my name go forward. The company ran a group selection at their head office. I was quite keen by the time I arrived and was looking forward to seeing some of the directors. But what a fiasco! I should think they made nearly every mistake in the book. These group selections aren't always a good idea and most of us felt a little uncomfortable. Two people in the short list knew each other, for example, and were clearly embarrassed. They tried to be super-efficient, keeping us on the go all the time. We had tests, including a personality one, an open discussion, board interviews, and finally a group exercise! It was obvious that they had never run one of these before, and the topics were badly chosen and badly introduced. The board interview was a gem! It would have been funny, if the situation hadn't meant so much. Five directors lined themselves up on the other side of a massive board room table and within ten minutes they were all talking at once. I did my best – but it wasn't long before they didn't need me at all! Needless to say, I wrote them a note as soon as I got home and withdrew. I hadn't realized before how dismally a firm of consultants can be let down by their clients later. In all fairness, they did warn me, but I didn't think that any board of directors would be quite so ham-fisted, these days!

The other firm – Easdale's – was as different as chalk from cheese. Their letters were almost pure Victoriana! Masses of medallions, heavily embossed parchment paper. I'm enclosing the one inviting me to the interview: needless to say, they gave me hardly any notice and coincided with my visit to France – which I had already told him about. Poor Ms Higgins! She changed the date, of course, amid profuse apologies.

I quite enjoyed my 'interview' with her – she's retiring at Christmas – a nice old welfare type who hasn't a clue about modern personnel practice. Her arrangements for expenses were equally Victorian, and when I pointed this out you'd have thought she had to pay me out of her own pocket! She didn't really interview me at all – just let me ask questions and see the place, which suited me very well. Her secretary seemed pretty efficient and the department has a useful nucleus of established routines, records and procedures.

Afterwards I was interviewed by two of the directors. It's an old family firm which has just been handed over to the next generation. Jack Easdale, the new managing director, is in his thirties, Cambridge and Harvard, and he certainly knows where he's going. It's not exclusively family and there's a chance of a seat on the board in a couple of years. I was rather surprised that they allowed Alison Higgins to handle the initial interviews, but the managing director said he wanted any newcomer to have a clear picture of the present position – and didn't want to hurt Alison's feelings.

Anyway, we got on very well together and I've now accepted the job. It's a gamble, I know, but it should give me plenty to do for quite a time. Of course, it will mean moving away from London, but I'll be back in the country at last, and there's an excellent repertory theatre about 10 miles away. And it will be wonderful to escape commuting every day!

Kindest regards,
Joan

Consultants' advertisement

Group Personnel Manager

Food Industry

for a group with 5 factories in S London, E Anglia,
Yorkshire and SW Scotland employing about 4,000 people.
This is a new appointment based at Head Office in London.
The Group Personnel Manager will be responsible to the
Managing Director. He/she will advise the Board on all
personnel matters, initiate and introduce progressive
personnel techniques and assist all managers to deal
effectively with their personnel problems.
Candidates, men or women, age 35 to 45, should be
graduates, preferably members of the IPM, and must be
trained and qualified personnel specialists now holding a
senior appointment in a group operating sophisticated
personnel techniques. Starting salary £30,000+ with
prospects of directorship. Non-contributory pension
scheme.
Please write to A B Connell, quoting P 3456 and stating
how each requirement is met.

Advertisement from personnel magazine

Group Personnel Manager

Company The Easdale Textile Company Ltd has seven factories in Yorkshire and Lancashire employing over 5,000.

Job The Group Personnel Manager will take over from the Personnel Superintendent who is due to retire at the end of the year. The personnel department (est. 1943) covers recruitment, welfare and sports facilities, pensions and sickness benefits, industrial relations and general personnel services. The Group Personnel Manager's immediate job will be to review personnel policies and practices and to extend the service throughout the entire group. Staff for the department includes five personnel officers. Canteens, security and cleaners all report through their departmental heads to the Group Personnel Manager.

Remuneration Starting salary subject to negotiation but not less than £35,000 p.a. plus profit sharing. Life assurance scheme and other benefits including share option scheme.

Applicants Should have a university degree and preferably have attended a one year full time course in personnel management. Should have at least ten years' experience of personnel work. Personal qualities are important.

To apply Write in the first instance to Ms A. Higgins marking the envelope 'Private and Confidential.'

THE EASEDALE TEXTILE CO LTD
BRADFORD, YORKS.

Letter from Easedale Textile Co Ltd

2 August 1990

Dear Ms Beresford,

Further to our communication of 26 July, in which we acknowledged yours of the 21st instance, we have much pleasure in inviting you to attend for interview at 2 30 on Thursday next, 8 August. We enclose a voucher for your return rail fare; a subsistance allowance will be paid according to the enclosed schedule.

I look forward to the pleasure of making your acquaintance.

Yours truly,
A HIGGINS
Personnel Superintendent

Extract from consultant's interview

— Now, Ms Beresford, would you tell me about the range of your personnel experience, starting with what led you into personnel work in the first place. As fully as you like, I won't interrupt unless I'm not clear on something.

— Right! I first thought about going into personnel work during my final year at university when I made arrangements to attend the one-year course. I didn't know much about it then, but it seemed as if it might be an interesting field to work in; a developing field that should give considerable scope for development. These ideas were confirmed later, although some of my idealism has now gone and I think I see things rather more realistically. I don't think my motives 'do gooding', although there was probably a small element of that at the time. I still believe that management is only just beginning to learn how best to organize itself so that it gets the full cooperation of its employees, both individually and collectively. Do you follow me?

— Yes, I understand perfectly.

— Well, I got my first job through the advice of my tutor. (Here I outlined my training and duties in my first appointment.)

— Looking back, do you think that your training might have been improved in any way?

– Oh yes, undoubtedly. The firm had had few people like myself and didn't quite know how to use us.

– Can you be more specific? In what ways did the training fall down?

– Over such things as guiding me so that I made the most of my time in a department. My training supervisor was a good man, but he didn't know enough, I fancy, either about personnel work or my needs, and so it amounted to learning by exposure, rather than giving me an aspect – or several aspects – to investigate, and then report back and discuss them. Also, my one-year course had given me a theoretical appreciation of personnel work, but now I had to see things through the other end of the telescope, as it were. It was a valuable background but at the time it was difficult to make the two compatible.

– How would you overcome these problems, if you were running such a course yourself Ms Beresford?

– I'd make a number of changes. For a start, I should want to know – as clearly as possible – what job trainees are likely to be given at the end of the training period. I suppose that sounds obvious, but it needs emphasizing. Also, I would give them an early taste of the ultimate job, if possible, so that they get an overall impression of what is involved and, at the same time, realize where their weaknesses lie, what experience is needed to get and so on. I think you need to have a clear picture of all the requirements an individual has, and to plan the course accordingly. If the person in question is a graduate, he or she will have been taught to examine problems from first principles, to subject them to detailed analysis and then to weigh other people's interpretations and, finally, to make up his or her own mind, arguing from evidence available. I would try to enable graduates to apply their trained minds to the industrial situation, giving as much information as can be digested, so that as problems are examined, they realize their own deficiencies. Then, special periods of attachment would be arranged, to fill in the gaps and so on. Lastly, when the graduate had acquired a fairly comprehensive picture of the total personnel function and of its problems, we could examine together how

best to match company demands with his or her own interests and preferences.
— That's fine. When referring to your first job on your application form, you mentioned an interest in shift work. Could you tell me a little more about this?

Commentary

Joan Beresford is not a model personnel manager. Nor would she think of herself as a model candidate, but a lot can be learned from her experience of changing her job. At executive level, the selection process is most obviously a two-way affair with a series of judgements and decisions being made by both parties. The candidate goes through a deliberate process of assessing the job and the company at each stage and she consciously weighs up whether she is sufficiently interested to proceed further. Her mental processes run parallel to whether to accept the job when an offer is made; and on her decision depends the outcome of all the recruiter's efforts. It is important, therefore, to understand what is likely to influence her favourably or unfavourably at each stage of the recruitment and selection procedure.

First, she is unlikely to be out of work. Secondly, she is not prepared to prejudice her present job or embarrass her employer by allowing it to become known that she is looking for another job. Indeed, she may not be actively doing so. More frequently she will be keeping her eyes open in case an attractive opportunity comes along, but without having made a firm decision about when or even whether she will move to another company. However, she is likely to have a fairly clear view of what might interest her. The next appointment she takes must seem to be a positive step towards the fulfilment of her career ambitions and must be free of what she regards as limitations in her present job.

Advertisements are scrutinized thoughtfully by Joan Beresford (and by most other executives). She will be disinclined to apply unless she sees some *prima facie* evidence that the advertised appointment might, on balance, represent an improvement over her present one. Her eyes are on the future as well as on the present. Before she will put herself forward as a candidate, she wants to feel reasonably assured that the job is one which she would like to have. It is the recruiter's task to supply Joan Beresford, as far as possible, with the desired information and to prompt her to take the first step by putting her in the right frame of mind. Once again, the starting point must be the job/person specification; and, in addition, the recruiter must consider how much background information about the company should be conveyed in order to present a clear picture of the size and scope of that job and of the context in which it is to be performed. The draft advertisement (assuming that the job is to be advertised) must be double-checked by the recruiter before it is released for publication. It will certainly be taken to pieces by the Joan Beresfords at whom it is being directed. The job title may not be suitable for the advertisement heading if it fails to convey accurately to an outsider the real nature of the work and the appropriate level of seniority. It should not be taken for granted that it will do so, since job titles can be notoriously misleading. The job dimensions can be indicated by factual references to, for example, the number of employees, proposed salary for the appointment, company turnover and growth rate etc. The advertisement should contain some such measurements to enable the potential candidate to judge whether the job is bigger or smaller than the job he or she is already doing. Salary is, of course, one such measurement but it is not the only relevant one nor is it the only motivating factor. However, the reader who is left with no clue about whether the job will carry a higher or lower salary than he or she is currently receiving may hesitate to apply. If the salary is published it must be realistically in line with the current market value for the type of candidate being sought. The company which recruits infrequently at management level may be wide of the mark, unless its salary structure is attuned sensitively to outside salary trends. Consultants are better placed in this respect because of their up to date knowledge of prevailing salaries and they can withhold the client's identity at the advertising stage, if it cannot be published safely in conjunction with the salary which is to be offered.

Managerial candidates also want to be assured explicitly that no information will be disclosed about any applications they make. Executives are more willing than is sometimes supposed to complete application forms provided that the questions asked are relevant and they have already been told enough about the job to be seriously interested in finding out more. In doing so, they like to feel that their application forms do full justice to what they can offer as individuals and an open-ended autobiographical section goes some way towards meeting that need, as well as providing the selector with useful clues about the candidates' attitudes and personal backgrounds. On the other hand many executives today have a well prepared curriculum vitae which not only gives the future 'track record' and personal details but also reveals what the individual considers to be of significance. If carefully studied a curriculum vitae can yield as much information – or more – than an application form but it is not so easy to compare the candidates point for point.

At the interview, the candidate will expect to be given ample opportunity to ask questions. Much can be learned from the questions asked and from the way they are put; and failure to raise certain points may also be significant. Typically, each interview will last for an hour or longer and the candidate will usually have to undergo more than one. The selector is not only concerned with finding out what the candidate knows, but also with probing the reasons for present attitudes and past behaviour. It is unreasonable to expect executives to turn up for interview at the drop of a hat. They have forward commitments in their present jobs and cannot cancel meetings or business engagements at short notice. Unless given at least 10 days' notice, they may find it difficult to attend.

The candidate will form his or her own impression of the interviewer. The skilled interviewer will earn respect, as well as finding out much more about the candidate. When dealing with candidates for senior positions, the untrained interviewer, relying on impromptu remarks and subjective conclusions, is at a marked disadvantage and can be fooled by a candidate who knows much more about the interview situation than he or she does. Joan Beresford was given a rough ride in the first job for which she was considered and she had good reason to withdraw her application. Few employers make so many mistakes at the same time – but it is surprising how many are made. Some boards of directors seem fond of forming themselves into interviewing panels and fail to see the clumsy and forbidding picture of themselves which they present to the shortlisted executives. Even the most ardent applicants might be daunted by the curious, and often atypical scenes enacted before them. Companies sometimes forget in their enthusiasm to try out modern selection techniques that group selection programmes require careful and skilful planning; and even then, an embarrassing situation can arise if the candidates are known to each other.

Not infrequently, an executive will have to move house before accepting another job and will not rush into this without weighing carefully all the implications. A partner's attitude and preferences can tip the balance. The risk of disrupting children's education can be a major obstacle. Before accepting the offer of an appointment, the successful candidate will weigh many factors in the balance including the social and financial costs of moving. Increased salary can be a powerful inducement – but the main attraction will often centre on the immediate challenge presented by the job and by the future prospects it offers. Candidates for managerial appointments are discriminating in the comparisons they make between one job and another. It is to the longer term advantage of the prospective employer, as well as themselves, that they should know about and accept the possible snags before tackling a new job rather than discover them afterwards.

Joan Beresford, as our *alter ego*, can now be allowed to retire gracefully from the limelight, but we should not forget how we might have reacted had we been in her shoes. Recall for a moment the most recent occasion on which your company sought to fill an executive appointment and consider how things looked from the viewpoint of an intelligent and experienced candidate. What impressions of your company were created by:

(i) the wording and layout of the advertisement?
(ii) the style of correspondence and application form?
(iii) the professional skill of the interviewer?
(iv) the organization of the short list procedures?
(v) the presence of your managerial colleagues and by their informal conversations over lunch?

Was the job filled – in spite of the quite unnecessary hazards which existed?

The director

Tom had retired early. He still had a twinge of conscience whenever he played golf midweek (it's the old work ethic, he told his wife). One Sunday evening he received a call from one of his former managers, Jack Underwood.

 — Hallo, Tom. Any chance you could spare me an half an hour sometime? There's a little problem I'd like to talk over with you – in strict confidence, of course.
 — Hallo, Jack, how nice to hear from you! Of course I'd be delighted to be a listening ear. Why don't you bring your golf clubs and I can thrash you at the same time! What day would suit you?
 — What a nice idea! I could manage any day to suit you. I'm still on the books of the old firm but technically I'm redundant now that we have sold the company.

Poor Jack; he had been one of Tom's best managers and had been put in charge of a small electronics company the group had acquired. He knew it would not all be plain sailing, but what had gone wrong? He put in a call to his old chairman; the subsidiary was making substantial losses and, although Jack had worked like a demon (it was he who had discovered the discrepancies), the group didn't have the cash to put things right. They had managed to sell the assets, but there was no other slot left for Jack. They were hoping, of course . . .

Jack was nervous and fluffed his first tee shot, but he gradually settled down and they had a passable round of golf. They discussed Jack's plight between holes, the effect on his wife, Mary, and the two children at boarding school. The group had treated him generously so he had a bit of time to look around. They had also paid for him to go to a firm of outplacement consultants. Jack had been to see them the previous week.

 — I'm glad I'm not paying; they charge an arm and a leg! Still, they seem to know what they are talking about and are very professional. You know, I haven't been for an interview since I left Cambridge and things have changed a lot in the meantime. I didn't like being squeezed into one of their

standard c.v.'s. I know what I would think from the other
side of the table. It leaves you neatly filleted, but all your
individuality is stripped out. I shall go along with it, as I
suppose they know best. What do you think, Tom? Any
advice you've got to give me? I wondered if you would put
in a word for me if the opportunity arises and act as one of
my referees?

Tom gave his advice, suggesting several firms he might approach
on Jack's behalf. 'I'd like that. Gives me an excuse to ring up
some of my old buddies and perhaps cadge a good meal or two!'

Jack worked hard responding to advertisements and writing
directly to a long list of headhunters and to the chairmen of some
targeted companies. There was some duplication, but he didn't
think that mattered. The outplacement company gave him secretarial help and they had a very good reference library. He saw
the counsellor several times and gradually sharpened his skills.

One of the first positive responses came from a firm of headhunters – from one of their research assistants.

— Mr Jack Underwood? My name is Debbie and I work for a
   well-known firm of executive search consultants (she gave
   their name and he remembered sending them his c.v.). We
   have your c.v. and there is an assignment we are working
   on that might be of interest.
— Fine, tell me more.
— Well, I can't reveal the name of our client at this stage, but
   I can tell you that they have a turnover of about £100 million
   and are in the electronics business.

Jack's memory bank worked overtime. £100M? that narrowed
it down to . . . he'd heard that they were in trouble over that
contract . . . or it could be . . . ?

— Are they manufacturers or simply assemblers and distribu-
   tors?
— They manufacture on two sites, one in Scotland and the
   other in the North of England.

That narrowed it down!

— Is it Microsystems of Renfrew?
— Er, I can't say.

Hole in one! He grinned. They were a tough company, but he could be interested if the job and the package was right. It might mean moving North; he wondered how Mary would react . . .

— What's the job and what are they offering?
— The job is as MD of their Nantwich operation and the package is negotiable.
— Can you give me any idea? I was on £60K basic at Swindon Electronics.
— That shouldn't be a problem. Can I make an appointment for you to see our Mr Alun Jones?
— Why not? I'm not sure about the company, but I'd like to meet Mr Jones.
— Shall we say this Friday at 10 o'clock?

That was a start, and not too bad. He doubted whether Mary would move North, but Mr Jones might know of something else.

He received a number of replies to his letters, some curt, some giving advice, some offering to see him briefly; many others did not reply at all. He'd set up a file and noted all these things down. He knew which firms he would not use in future. Several offered him 'a half-hour's chat'. They usually dealt with the electronics industry and were interested to get to know him against future assignments.

A hectic couple of months followed, during which he wrote many more letters, saw a number of consultants and companies, haunted the outplacement offices and kept his files rigorously up to date. He played a return match with Tom and reported progress.

— It's interesting to see things from the other side of the table. You know, I haven't been interviewed from scratch since my Cambridge days. It's surprising how much I had forgotten – dates and things – but they all came back with some skilful interviewing. But what a mixed bag! There are some right cowboys around and you see a different face of some household names when you are an applicant instead of a customer. Some are frighteningly badly managed and financially overstretched; the first whiff of a recession and they will go under.

— What do you mean by cowboys: recruitment agencies, companies or headhunters?

— All three. Some who call themselves search consultants are a disgrace. They've usually been set up by an ex-serviceman or junior line manager and bear a close resemblance to the popular image of estate agents. They put in the minimum effort, don't really know what they are talking about and have had no training in interviewing or selection techniques. Most of all they don't really know what it's like to sit in an MD's chair. Take E S & Partners; dingy, back-street offices, filing systems nonexistent, false bonhomie – ugh! They pretended that they knew all about me, but the only thing they referred to was the c.v. I had sent them. I was offered a glass of beer (and plastic cup) and the interviewer sat there with his feet on the desk and chewed a sandwich. He pushed across a copy of the report and accounts and a very brief job description the client company had obviously prepared and asked if I was interested and could he put my name forward! When I tried to ask some questions, he clearly hadn't read or understood the accounts and had never even visited the site or met the person I would report to. I was pretty short with him, I can tell you! Quite a good job and a well-known company. How the consultant had got the brief beats me; must know someone, I suppose.[1]

They were now at the 'nineteenth hole' enjoying a pint of the club's best bitter. Jack opened his Filofax.

— The professionals were as different as chalk from cheese. I made a few notes for future reference – thought they might help me to improve my own interviewing skills. Very good, quiet professional feel about the place and the staff; soon put you at your ease – a bit like your old office, Tom! For

[1] This is taken from the author's own experience!

example, one of the consultants – Rodney something or
other – and I sat around a small table with our cups of the
inevitable coffee and a small pile of brochures, reports and
accounts etc. We discussed the company and the brief in
outline and occasionally he would pull out a booklet to show
me a picture or to read a short paragraph. Not ostentatious,
but he clearly knew his way around them – which gives you
confidence. He talked frankly and confidentially for about
10 minutes, sketching in the background to the appointment
and why the company were going outside for some new
blood. I found this very helpful when talking about my own
experience later and it triggered a number of questions
which I guess revealed quite a lot about me and my grasp
of the real situation. There are problems there, but none I
couldn't handle with some good back-up. He then slipped
smoothly into my own background and probed deeply into
my experience. I can tell you, there wasn't much about me
that he didn't know by the time we had finished, but I didn't
mind as I felt it was worthwhile. He hardly ever looked at
my c.v. but had clearly memorized what it contained and
his note-taking was quite unobtrusive – not like one chap
who behaved like a copper: 'Everything you say will be
taken down and used in evidence against you.' He had
obviously taken the trouble to check me out beforehand.
He didn't say how he knew, but every so often he would
bring in a fact which I knew wasn't in my c.v. All done quite
subtly and almost unobtrusively. It put me on my guard as
I felt it wouldn't be easy to put one over on him. (Tom said
nothing; he had given his word to the consultant . . .)

– I made a note of some of his questions – if I'm not boring
you?

– Not at all, Jack; I'm fascinated.

– Here's one; when you were running the plant at Bristol, I
believe you made some major changes; how did you sell
these to the staff? (How did he know that we were having
trouble with the unions – a spin-off from the GCHQ affair
at Cheltenham?)

Here's another; from what you now know about the company and the brief, and drawing on your own experience,
what would be your initial strategy?

An MD's job is a lonely one. All advice you receive is bound to be slanted; how do you cope with that?
If you had your time again, and with the benefit of hindsight, would you have made any changes? If so, what?
What has been the pattern of your annual performance reviews? What areas did you mostly have to concentrate on? Did you make any changes? How exactly? And did they work? Can you give me an example?

– He didn't let you off the hook! Did you mind? Some might.
– No; because I felt he knew what he needed to find out. An MD's job is a highly critical one – both for the incumbent and the company. Failure can cost both of you dearly. With some interviewers you feel that they are simply prying; the good ones reveal their hand just sufficiently so that you know that it's as much to your advantage as it is theirs.
– Incidentally, it's a time-consuming business going for jobs. Thank goodness I've not got a job to hold down at the same time! A good interviewer can easily take a couple of hours and some want to see you several times. One company called me back six times – all at short notice – and then sent me a short note saying sorry without any word of explanation! The consultant was quite good and found out what went wrong. Would you believe it? They decided to promote one of their own people – felt it would take me too long to get to know the peculiarities of their business! Scared an outsider would uncover too much, I guess! But what a waste of time and money – for both of us.

Commentary

Recruiting a senior executive is a rare occurrence for most personnel managers. Without a cross sample of this segment of the population it is difficult to put people in 'rank order' and to compare like with like. Personnel directors of large groups do get an opportunity, but for many it makes sense to go to an outside consultant to whom the CE can talk freely, seeking unbiased advice and drawing on their wide experience. It is best, therefore, to choose a consultant who has personally held down a top job and seen a range of companies and knows from first hand that there is more than one way of tackling a problem. Such a consultant has to be taken into full confidence if the job is to be done thoroughly. He or she becomes an extension to the top team during the assignment and so 'face validity' is vital. So are confidentiality and trust.

If you are asked for your advice in handling a top appointment, how would you set about choosing a firm of consultants? Would you be helpful or critical? How would you monitor their performance? Would you give them the information they want – or make them find out for themselves? If your CE is 'a difficult cuss with a short fuse', would you back off and try to please or would you have the courage to 'beard the lion in his den'? Recruitment is a two-way affair; both the company and the individual need to know as much as they reasonably can about the other before an appointment is made. It's no use saying later 'I didn't like to ask the old man' – when the new recruit walks out on his first day after at last seeing some true management accounts. After all, you would do the same – wouldn't you?

3

Assessing the candidate

Summary

Earlier chapters have emphasized that recruitment and selection work should be thought of as a matching process. This concept is so fundamental that no apology is made for repeating it. Having assessed the demands of the job, we know what attributes we are looking for and possess in the person specification a yardstick against which we can assess the suitability of the candidate. The next practical step is to decide the methods by which we shall recognize the presence or absence in individual candidates of these attributes. Our immediate aim is to narrow the field of candidates by progressively eliminating those who do not measure up to the person specification. We may also wish to see whether any of those about to be eliminated should be considered for a different job.

Matching implies that candidate requirements which can be measured have been identified in the job and that we know how to measure people in terms of those attributes. Tools and techniques which go a long way towards doing this have been developed during the past 50 years, but they are far from perfect. They are of little use if applied by an unskilled person; nor can satisfactory results be expected if they are applied slavishly to every candidate for every job. All assessment techniques presuppose competence on the part of the user, and that competence comes only from training and practical experience. This is true especially of the most commonly used technique of all: the interview. It is a curious fact that almost everyone prides themselves on being good judges of people. Only bitter personal disappointment seems capable of destroying this self-deception; any reasonable foundation for it disappeared half a century ago, when classic research studies exposed it as a myth.

Demonstrably, some people are capable of becoming more proficient than others at selection work, so the assessor needs to have been carefully selected. The role of an interviewer demands sensitivity to the process of human interaction, and adaptability to each individual interviewed. We require sympathy and, at the same time, objectivity in order to weigh up a complex range of evidence and reach a firm conclusion. By their nature, other techniques of assessment obviously call for specific training before they can be used at all. The selector has to exercise skill and discretion in applying them, since their value varies considerably with the type of candidate being assessed. In particular, they must be acceptable to the candidate and this, too, varies with age and with type of occupation.

The selection techniques used most widely in industry at present are:

(i) the application form
(ii) the interview
(iii) group selection methods
(iv) psychological tests

Each is discussed in detail later in this chapter and the table on pages 94–5 gives a general indication of the points to bear in mind when considering their use. As a guide, the appropriateness of these four techniques has been summarized in relation to half a dozen different categories of potential candidates. The range of techniques available to be used depends on the professional competence of the selector and will take into account:

(a) the attributes to be assessed and the degree of accuracy required
(b) type and level of appointment
(c) age distribution of candidates
(d) probable acceptability of the different methods
(e) time available
(f) comparative costs

As with any skilled worker, the selectors must know when to use each tool, how to apply it and what its inherent strengths and limitations are. To take the analogy further, consider the degree of finish required, since this influences choice of a coarse or a fine selection device at each stage of the process.

Application forms

Summary

Well-constructed application forms are one of the best selection tools. This is because they compare like with like; they are factual; and the selector is unbiased by the presence of the person. The questions asked should be relevant and within the capability of the applicant. The layout of the form should make it easy to read, easy to respond to, and give adequate space for people with long addresses and large handwriting. Company administrative or selector's graphics/boxes should be kept to a minimum as these are offputting or may reveal the selector's hand. If the design follows the seven or the five point plan, application forms are easier to use as a basis for interviewing. Some companies produce a new form for each job; most have three basic ones – for school leavers, for practical jobs and for technical/managerial jobs. Information in the application form can be matched point for point with the person specification; those lacking some essential requirement are immediately rejected and the rest interviewed according to the strength of their relevant experience/qualifications.

Assessment does not start with the interview. For many jobs it is perfectly possible, and often essential, to eliminate the majority of the applicants without an interview. In carrying out these preliminary stages of assessment, the selector relies largely on documentary evidence.

Initial letters of application vary widely in the amount of relevant information they contain. Much depends on how the advertisement itself was phrased. If the job was described fairly fully and the candidate requirements were stated in specific terms, the resultant letters of application should contain factual information about the candidate. In such cases, it will often be possible to eliminate between one-third and one-half of the applicants on the strength of their initial letters. By contrast, fewer replies to a woolly advertisement can be eliminated without serious risk of losing potentially worthwhile candidates.

The Principal Assessment Techniques
A general guide to their use

Types of Candidate	Application Form	Initial Interview	Psychological Tests	Group Discussion
1 School leavers (and aged up to 18)	Valuable. Should highlight family background and occupations, school performance, examination results (external), hobbies and interests. Keep simple. Avoid asking for irrelevant information.	Need encouragement and sensitive handling, as not used to expressing themselves in a formal situation. Start interview at factual level based on application form, and develop depth questioning later. Expect apparent conflicts in interest and personality patterns at this age. *Typical time: 20–40 mins*	Useful. Can reveal latent as well as actual ability. The general factor 'g' wil often 'swamp' other factors; exceptions are spatial and (some) attainment tests.	Only useful with the well above average. (Likely to opt out.)
2 Shop floor operatives, clerical grades	Keep factual and simple. Allow less space for school and plenty of space for work history. Frequency and pattern of job changes is very important. Can omit schooling before age 11, also family traditions, but ask for names of relatives or friends who are employees.	Use a formal, well-structured pattern with direct questions and occasional probes. Explore range of experience and peaks of attainment; also how well they have fitted into other companies. Photographs and display of products make communications easier. *Typical time: 15–30 mins*	Rarely useful or acceptable if aged over 25, except to assess suitability for promotion or retraining. 'Work sample' tests can be valuable if properly devised and conducted, but coordinated dexterity inclined to be highly particularized.	Rarely worth using.
3 Supervisors, senior clerical, senior technicians	Straightforward and easy to complete. Emphasis on school, subsequent academic achievements, range of work experience, responsible roles held at work and outside.	Fairly formal, structured pattern. Probe gaps in application form (if any) and exact nature of experience. Allow at least five minutes for candidate to ask questions. *Typical time: 20–30 mins*	Depends on age and experience. Can be useful when entirely new work to be done, extensive training involved or first supervisory appointment.	For some supervisory posts. Clues to personality factors and management approach likely to be adopted. Guide to breadth of understanding of the problems about to be met.

4 *Graduates*	Carefully designed form should highlight family background, academic and social activities at both schools and university (to show rate of development), participation in university societies. Longer term ambitions may sometimes be more important than shorter term goals.	Flexible pattern and needs delicate handling. Treat as a vocational guidance interview. Encourage them to talk about ambitions and introspections. Relate proven ability and personality to ambitions, in order to judge realistic career pattern. Use open questions and probe. *Typical time: 30–45 mins*	Use general intelligence tests to determine the extent to which they use their ability. This may be masked by (a) over participation in student affairs, (b) choice of subjects to suit a narrow ability, (c) tremendous effort expended to achieve an average result.	Very useful. Guide to personality and ability to apply academic training to real-life problems.
5 *Professionally qualified executives*	Design to provide a running outline of home background, schooling qualifications, training and interests. Place emphasis on range and depth of experience (including supervisory roles), self-analysis, and career aims. A good C.V. may yield all the information needed prior to interview.	Determine the rate and direction of career and personal development by open questions, self-analysis, comparative questions and probing. Pattern of development before 21 particularly important. Exactly similar experience often less important than grasp of principles and good record of application to other tasks. Allow 15 mins for candidate to ask questions. *Typical time: 30–60 mins*	Not always acceptable. Useful, particularly if in doubt about trainability or administrative ability when 'g' tests coupled with verbal (v:ed) tests can provide additional evidence.	Useful and generally acceptable. Guide to strong attitudes, how well likely to fit in, and ability to apply past experience to new problems.
6 *Senior managers*	Administer discriminatingly. C.V. may be adequate for first-stage screening in many cases. Avoid asking for unnecessary duplication. Candidate resistance to form-filling not as great an obstacle as generally supposed, if handled tactfully. Use same form as 5, occasionally with specific questions added.	Very flexible approach needed. Discussion interspersed with probing, *or* information about job/company, followed by 'interview', followed by discussion. *or* rapid appraisal of basic facts (to fill in gaps and get a balanced picture) followed by discussion of experience and aims. *Typical time: 45–75 mins*	Unlikely to be acceptable in some cases although now becoming used more widely. Effective application of intelligence and administrative aptitude can be assessed by 'g' and v:ed tests. Applied intelligence, e.g. 'critical thinking', and personality tests can reveal quality of judgement and perceived personality traits.	Sometimes not acceptable, as candidates may fear face to face confrontation with others could jeopardize their present positions. Information sessions, individual or group, may yield sociometric or interaction information not available in normal interview.

The application form is a basic selection instrument. It is much more valuable than is generally realized. If carefully designed and interpreted, it can provide a wealth of information about a candidate. Conversely, it will prove to be a blunt instrument if these conditions are not fulfilled. Commonly it is misused. Its principal purpose is to ask pertinent questions and elicit relevant information, thus enabling the selector to identify candidates who correspond closely to the person specification. Subsequently, it can serve as a framework around which the interview may be built. Lastly, it can be kept as a record of the employee's background, but this is its least important function.

Unfortunately, an application form is liable to become regarded as part of a standard routine. The procedure tends to obscure the real purpose. There is no point in asking people to fill in a form if their original letters reveal that they fail to meet one or more of the essential requirements of the job. Similarly, there is little point in inviting someone to attend an interview (and to forfeit a day's work in doing so) if careful study of their career record would show that they are unlikely to be suitable for the job. The candidate's time is valuable too.

The application form is therefore basically a method of asking and answering questions by correspondence. The selector should already have a clear idea from the person specification of the criteria by which candidates will be differentiated. The application form needs to be designed with those criteria in mind. Obviously what the selector wants to know and what the candidate has to say, and is willing to disclose, varies widely according to the type of job to be filled and the age group of the candidates. Seen in these terms, a standard form used for all jobs must be inefficient, since the questions it asks will be irrelevant in some respects to most candidates and the manner and sequence in which they are posed may also be inappropriate. The application form is too valuable a selection instrument to be abused in this way.

In the medium-sized company at least three different versions of the application form will be needed. They will have been especially designed for recruiting different types of employees such as factory and clerical workers; school leavers; and professionally qualified staff and managers. In the larger company, additional variations may be used, according to the range of occupations covered and the scale of recruitment undertaken. When recruiting managerial grades, the application form can be given an even sharper cutting-edge by the addition of several supplementary questions specifically designed to probe the relevance of the candidate's experience. Contrary to popular belief, this improves the form's acceptability to candidates as well as strengthening its technical efficiency, since the relevance of the questions makes it immediately apparent that the form is being administered in an intelligent and purposeful way. Theoretically, the form should always be tailor-made to suit the particular appointments to be filled, but in practice most personnel officers find that three or four basic versions are adequate for most of their recruitment work.

The application form should therefore be administered sensitively and sensibly. We need to bear in mind that many people have a healthy dislike of form-filling and are disinclined to perform this laborious task. A candidate is more likely to complete the application form if a covering letter explains that the initial letter has been read and that the first hurdle has already been surmounted as forms are not being distributed automatically to everyone who has applied. A common practice is to grade all the initial applications into three categories of unsuitable, possible and interview. The 'unsuitables' are eliminated immediately; the 'possibles' are sent an application form in order to obtain additional evidence about their strengths and weakneses; whilst the 'interviews' are sent a letter inviting them to an interview and requesting them to return the completed application form when confirming the date of the proposed meeting. The latter procedure is normally used for only the small minority of applicants who conform most closely to the person specification. It reduces the risk that they will lose interest in the appointment, but the application form is still needed as a framework for the interview. It is prudent to carry out a periodic spot-check of the proportion of forms which are in fact completed, as a low ratio may indicate that the form is either badly-constructed or is being administered clumsily.

The table on pages 98–9 may serve as a check-list of possible contents when designing application forms. It should not be regarded as a model, nor is it suggested that every application form should include every item. On the contrary, the essence of a good application form is that it is constructed to suit the particular

The Application Form
A check list of possible coverage

Subject		Observations
Personal particulars	Full name Address (permanent or temporary) Telephone number (home and business) Date of birth Marital status: dependants Height: weight: state of health	
Family background	Relations employed by the company Parental occupations Occupations of brothers and sisters	Provides clues to opportunities afforded. For adults, an open-ended question about traditional occupations or professions is preferable.
Education – general	Schools attended: name and type Examinations: subjects, grades, dates School offices held Scholarships, prizes	Education since 11 may be sufficient in the case of older applicants
– further	College/university: course taken Examinations: subjects, grades, dates Offices held. Extra-curricula activities	
Vocational training	Apprenticeship/articles/special training Nature and place of training Professional qualifications: date qualified, present grade of membership Languages: oral, written; degree of fluency	Note whether full time or part time study.

Employment history	Complete chronological record of all jobs held with dates Nature and scale of duties, and to whom responsible Name and address of employer Starting and finishing salary Reasons for leaving	Allow sufficient space for present (or last) job to be described more fully. For senior appointments, brief account of significant achievements. Names of referees are better obtained at interview.
Leisure interests	Hobbies; leisure pursuits Membership of societies; offices held	Establish the range, depth and persistence of what the applicant chooses to do of his/her own free will. A check-list can be provided for completion by school leavers. For senior appointments, can be included in an autobiographical account.
Application	Type of job sought Date of any previous application When free to start work	
Self-assessment	Likes and dislikes Special job interests Future aims and ambitions	Should be towards the end of the form. For senior appointments, applicants may be asked to outline how well they meet the requirements set out in the advertisement.

circumstances, and these vary from job to job and from company to company.

In general, it is better to arrange the items in chronological sequence, but grouping together all aspects of education and training. This is done primarily to simplify the applicant's task, but it also assists the selector by making it easier to identify patterns. Administrative codes and symbols should be kept to the minimum, as they are distracting and may be viewed with suspicion. The layout should allow an adequate amount of space for each item and cater for those with large handwriting. Lines are a great help to many people, especially those unaccustomed to writing. Since the purpose is to elicit relevant information, it is sensible to examine periodically a sample of completed forms in order to check whether the required information is being obtained in a coherent and economical way.

It has been emphasized in earlier chapters that a principal aim is to compare the demands of the job with the candidate's capacities and inclinations by means of a technique such as the seven-point plan or the five-point plan. A good deal of the candidate information to be sought under these systems can be deduced from a well-constructed application form and classified under these seven (or five) headings. The form cannot tell the whole story about the candidate but, carefully interpreted, it can reveal some of the salient features. In particular, it can provide some provisional evidence and clues concerning the applicant's:

> biographical data and personal circumstances
> career pattern and attainments
> powers of self-expression
> range and depth of interests
> intelligence and special aptitudes
> behaviour patterns and preferences

When evaluating a completed application form, it is customary to read first the factual sections, to see whether the candidate meets all of the *essential* requirements in the person specification. There is nothing to be gained by spending time on a detailed evaluation of an applicant if it is immediately apparent that they lack one of the essential attributes. They must be disqualified from further consideration for that particular job, although if other jobs are to be filled as well, this form may repay closer study against different person specifications later.

On completion of this first reading, the applicant can be placed into one of three provisional categories corresponding broadly to 'unsuitable', 'possible' and 'probable'. The word provisional is used advisedly. A second and more analytical study of the application form is needed to select for interview those candidates who correspond most closely to the person specification. The real skill in interpretation and deduction comes into play at this point. A synoptic view of the applicant and of the job now being done will already have been acquired from the first inspection of the application form. The more difficult step is to assess how and why the person concerned has developed in reaching his or her present position. In doing so, we postulate the hypothesis that the pattern of people's previous behaviour can provide some clues to the way they are likely to behave in the future. When assessing older applicants this hypothesis can be relied on with greater assurance than when dealing with younger candidates. It should also be noted that persistent characteristics may be more significant than isolated occurrences.

With practice, much more than appears on the surface can be learnt about applicants by considering how they performed in previous situations, for example at school, at work and in society. The use they have made of opportunities, the handicaps overcome, the extent to which they have proved themselves compatible in different social groupings, are some of the trends and tendencies which may be apparent from past records. Taken together, they can serve as valuable guides when considering jobs for which applications have been received. It is important to bear in mind that even a well-designed application form will not contain all the parts of the jigsaw puzzle we are attempting to piece together. Inevitably there will be some gaps in our knowledge, perhaps vital ones, which remain unfilled. This additional information will have to be gleaned later by tests or by personal interview. Even so, these tentative deductions about the candidate are of considerable value especially as they are made without the interplay of personalities which occurs in the face to face situation of the interview. On the strength of these tentative conclusions some candidates will be eliminated. The remainder will meet the selector who has a clear idea of what else is needed in order to find out about them. An analysis of the application form has enabled the selector to note the areas for which further exploration is necessary and the selector will concentrate on those particular points when planning and conducting interviews. Thus the best use of the time available will be made and interviews will be correspondingly more efficient.

It has become a feature of recent years, perhaps as a result of American influence, that most managers and professional people have a curriculum vitae in their files which they update from time to time. Many of these have been 'professionally' produced and reasonably accurately convey the basic facts about the subject – education, qualifications, career summary – and as such are useful to the selector. However, people are more than the sum total of their parts and the risk is that c.v.s produced in this way clinically delete individual personality features of the individual, thereby removing the most valuable feature of a self-produced curriculum vitae – a reflection of the writer as conceived by him- or herself. Many recipients so dislike these standard curriculum vitae that they consign them to the waste paper basket; which is a grave injustice to the individual who has paid for advice and help. They are of value in making a quick evaluation and deciding whether to take things further; but in the author's view, no more than that.

The interview[1]

Summary

Interviewing is the most widely used selection tool; it is also the most abused and the least reliable in the hands of the untrained. It is used for its flexibility; the need to meet face to face; and because it has high 'face validity' (i.e. both parties accept it, like it and believe it works!). Trained interviewers know what they can

---

[1] Throughout this publication, the word *interview* relates specifically to the *employment* interview. There are many other circumstances in which a person may be 'interviewed' where the information getting/attitude revelation techniques used in selection interviewing are directly applicable. Most managers 'interview' every day in a wide variety of situations and do not realize that the application of sound interviewing techniques can help them in their day to day work (e.g. discipline, promotion, salary review, counselling, dismissal, vocational guidance etc).

assess with reasonable accuracy and don't attempt the impossible. They ensure that the setting is right, that candidates are sufficiently reassured before probing too hard; they know how to help the candidate to respond to difficult questions and to separate fact from gloss. They make optimum use of the time available. Interviewing is a two-way process, so they ensure that the candidate has sufficient information and leaves feeling that he/she has had a fair hearing and that there has been no overt discrimination.

Interviewing can produce abominable results. It frequently does; but the fault usually lies in the interviewer rather than in the assessment method. Interviewing is an everyday occurrence and is the most widely used assessment technique; it is part of the popular vocabulary; it looks easy, and everyone is inclined to believe they are good at it. Therein lies the danger and the confusion. In practice, many so-called interviews consist of untrained employers talking generalities about jobs they have not analysed to would-be employees about whom they know little, and then deciding whether or not to offer them the job. In such unpropitious circumstances it would indeed be surprising if the predictive value of the interview were anything but poor.

Research studies have demonstrated time and time again that interviewing competence varies enormously, and that some people are very bad at it. Thus it has become fashionable in recent years to disparage the interview. This is no more helpful than condemning the technique of diagnostic examination in the field of medicine, on the grounds that the lay person has difficulty in telling measles from chickenpox! The registered medical practitioner recognizes the difference as a result of relevant training and experience; and the circumstances in which he or she works leave no option but to rely on diagnostic examinations, even though the technique as such depends on human judgement. So it is with the interview in industry. It is a necessary and unavoidable part of the selection process, because it fulfils other functions as well as being a convenient and acceptable method of assessing the candidate. Our efforts therefore should be directed towards improving the standards of interviewing, and this is the main theme of this chapter.

Objectives

The interviewer should have in mind constantly three main objectives. The first, and most obvious, is to establish whether the candidate is suitable for the job and, if not, in what particular job their talents could best be used to mutual advantage.

The second objective is to ensure that the candidates have an accurate picture of the job for which they are being considered. If he or she is a strong contender for the job, it is doubly important to provide a full understanding of what that job entails. It is pointless to gloss over aspects which the interviewer thinks may be unattractive. If, in fact, they are unattractive to that candidate, it is far better to withdraw at the preliminary interview rather than discover them later. A new employee who believes he or she has been misled is unlikely to stay in the job for long.

The third objective is to conduct the interview in such a manner that the candidate feels he or she has had a fair hearing, whether engaged or not. The interview itself assumes a high degree of importance in the minds of the prospective candidates. They are prone to feel acute disappointment if deprived of the opportunity to state their case in person and, if invited to an interview, approach it with high hopes. Their impressions of the company as well as of the job applied for are coloured by the way in which the interview is conducted.

Some basic faults

Most people who read this publication will readily accept that interviewing calls for skills which have to be learned, can be taught and should be based on research findings. Even so, few will have studied the research evidence for and against the interview, and some will be blissfully unaware that its validity as an assessment technique has been repeatedly challenged. Research studies have shown that some of the more prevalent weaknesses can be traced to:

Brief, unsystematic interviewing Conclusions are based on hunches rather than on facts, candidates being assigned preconceived classifications without examining all the relevant evidence. 'Prejudice is a great time saver – it enables you to form opinions without having to get the facts.'

Inadequate application forms Vital facts are likely to be missed or misconstrued. The interview may degenerate into an interrogation through relentless efforts to overcome this deficiency.

Interviewers unaware of their own limitations The assessment should be confined to those attributes which the interviewer can measure accurately and reliably. Ill-conceived attempts to isolate and assess such abstract qualities as honesty, conscientiousness, integrity etc may amount to little more than wild guesses. They are notoriously difficult to infer, even where the interviewer has made a careful reconstruction and analysis of the candidate's past behaviour in the context of specific situations.

Subjective spot-checks Answers to the interviewer's favourite questions are allowed to assume disproportionate weighting in the final assessment, even though they may not constitute a fair sample of each person's knowledge, or may not correlate with successful performance in that job.

Failure to establish rapport This is essentially a matter of communication and mutual trust. The significance of the candidates' words, allusions and social values have to be manifestly understood and respected, before they will confide further facts about themselves to the interviewer.

Interviewer talks too much As a general guide, interviewers should be speaking for less than one third of the time. You will usually learn more when listening and the interviewee talking!

Preparation for an interview

Before the interview begins, the interviewer should have studied all the available information about the candidate, and particularly the application form, so the task of assessment can be concentrated on fully. By its nature, interviewing is a time consuming process and, within reason, everything possible should be done to ensure the best use of the time available. A careful examination of what is already recorded will help the selector to plan the interview and to devote the greater part of the time to those aspects which need clarification or amplification.

To advocate that the interview should be planned at all strikes some people as undesirable, whilst others feel compelled to compile a long string of questions or a detailed check-list. Neither extreme is justified. A skeleton plan helps the interviewer to concentrate on observing the candidate and interpreting what is said, instead of frantically wondering what subject to raise next. It helps the interviewer to keep the discussion to the point and avoids the risk of embarrassing pauses. The skeleton plan should not be followed rigidly, but can be modified as the conversation progresses. The interview has to start somewhere; it has to be steered so that it covers the ground indicated in the person specification and it has to be brought tactfully to its close. To do this well requires considerable skill and practice. A detailed check-list can become a strait-jacket, but a brief note of particular facets to be explored and a few key phrases is invaluable, if not indispensable. A useful technique is to prepare on one sheet of paper a chronological analysis of the application to show concurrent activities – and gaps. Draw up an age scale – present age on the left-hand side. Divide the page vertically into four columns. In column 1 show career landmarks (change of job title, special projects tackled, change of job etc); in the second column education and training courses and results. Use the third column for any other specific activity or achievement (hobby, professional activity, outside work, date married and birth of children, illness etc) and in the final column note inconsistencies, points you are not clear about, for example 'four month gap'; 'why not complete the course – marriage?'; 'sideways move'; 'apparent drop in salary'; 'took drop to stay in town band?'

This preparation has another value. It facilitates the early establishment of rapport, by demonstrating to the candidate that the information supplied earlier has been studied and found to be of interest. Thus the candidate is encouraged to feel that what is said during the interview will also be considered worthy of interest. The subject of intra-personal communication is discussed more fully later in this chapter. It is relevant here in that the interviewer's preparation has enabled him to give the first clues to the level of communication which can be attained between two people who are strangers to each other. Conversely, rapport will be inhibited if the interviewer's early remarks or questions convey that he has either not read or not remembered what should have been apparent from the candidate's application form.

When an interview programme is being arranged, the times of candidates' arrivals should be carefully spaced so that waiting is kept to the minimum. Apart from considerations of courtesy, candidates are unlikely to do themselves justice if they have become nervous or irritated through being kept waiting. There is another and less altruistic reason. Interviewers are tempted to skimp their preparation if they know they are behind schedule and, in the resultant interview, may not do justice either to the candidate or to themselves.

The physical setting

In the normal course of events personnel officers will conduct interviews in their own offices. Some large companies set aside a number of small, quiet rooms furnished informally for this purpose. When a number of candidates from another part of the country are under consideration, it may be advantageous to arrange to see them at a hotel in that district. When doing so, a private room should be reserved. The practice of trying to interview across a luncheon table or in a public lounge is generally to be deplored. The candidate is made unnecessarily tense by the risk of being seen or overheard; and the interviewer will be unable to concentrate properly.

The physical setting has quite an important bearing on the degree of rapport which can be established. An office used for interviewing should be reasonably noise-proof and the furnishings should not be too distracting. Chairs should be so arranged that the interviewer does not appear to be dominating the candidate. With a little forethought, it is seldom necessary for the interviewer to address the candidate across an enormous desk, or from a higher chair, or to have artificial light blazing into the eyes of the guest. Documents which are not needed should be cleared away before the candidate enters the room. There should be complete freedom from telephone calls and other interruptions whilst the interview is in progress. If notes are to be made, the interviewer must arrange the seats at a sufficient distance so that the candidate will be unable to read what is written.

These arrangements are not advocated out of desire to pamper the candidate: they are essential if the interviewer is to do the job properly. Concentration is essential. Anyone who believes otherwise has not made a serious study of the subject.

Conducting the interview

A delicate balance has to be struck between formality and friendliness, between clinical examination and casual confidences entrusted to a sympathetic ear. Solemnity and impressiveness are regarded by some as being advantages of the selection board interview, whilst others urge that every interview should be conducted in a completely informal vein. To the candidate, both are unnatural and threatening. The interview should be conducted in an atmosphere which is 'known' and which seems favourable to both parties. Acknowledge the 'threat' but limit it by conveying to the candidate that they need not be afraid of admitting their own shortcomings. Explain, and mean, that everything is confidential. Be sympathetic and understanding, but always acknowledge the formal relationship and never take unfair advantage of the candidate.

It is fundamental that the candidate should be put at ease on entering the room. The interviewer's opening remarks are therefore of paramount importance. They inform the candidate how he or she is expected to respond and the amount of time set aside, in order to use the time to the maximum advantage and with the right degree of emphasis. They set the candidate at ease by providing an operational framework ('this is what I am aiming to do'), by motivating a free response and by setting the quiet, unhurried, sympathetic atmosphere. The candidate has a chance to get used to the interviewer's voice and to overcome some initial tension. The introduction should never be stereotyped and should be adjusted according to the type of person being interviewed.

The interview should start and finish at definite points of time. There is little time or need for casual chat. The interview should be terminated firmly by telling the candidate when he or she will be informed of the outcome and by a physical movement, such as standing up to help the candidate with his or her coat.

The flow of the discussion is largely in the hands of the interviewer, who must be in control of the situation throughout, however light may be his or her touch. If the interviewer expressed him/herself clearly at the outset, so that the candidate knows in advance what sort of response is expected of him, relevant answers to questions will usually be supplied. If this is not the case, the candidate can soon be directed back to the right lines. Simple praise (*'I was most interested in* . . . *'*) or blame (*'I'd rather we concentrated on* . . . *'*) will work wonders on the person who has wandered away from the point.

When learning to interview, some people find it difficult to move from one subject to another and feel compelled to interject 'Thank you very much' at the end of each answer. This is quite unnecessary and stresses the undesirable aspects of formality (e.g. it can destroy rapport). The good listener will always find a link question from among asides and comments on previous subjects (*'You mentioned just now that* . . . *Could you tell me a little more about* . . . *'*). A comparative question will frequently suffice, and, at the same time, introduce a demand for self-insight (*'How did that work compared with* . . . *'*) The interview should be closed by giving the candidate an opportunity to ask questions and to volunteer information which he or she feels has not been taken adequately into account. This can be achieved quite simply by asking *'Is there anything else you would like to know about this job?'* and by posing a question such as *'Are there any other important aspects you would like to raise?'*

Communication

Even experienced interviewers sometimes forget the physical, psychological and emotional difficulties of expressing oneself clearly in an ego-threatening situation. Experience, aims, motives, etc are expressed in words by some people for the first and last time in the interview situation. Personalized memories are hard to express in objective terms and harder still to recall at the drop of a hat. The typical applicant has a vocabulary of about 5,000 words (i.e. about 10 per cent of the English vocabulary) and so lacks the verbal equipment to say precisely what he or she means. They try to do so by analogy or by a series of apparently disjointed and often inadequate utterances. This must be allowed for by the interviewer. The candidate must be given time to reply and encouraged to express him/herself freely in revealing the framework of his/her life and thoughts.

If rapport is to be established and held throughout the interview, there must be empathy between the parties concerned. This is communicated through choice of phrase and manner, and particularly by the interviewer's words, emphasis and facial expressions. Communication between human beings is a process involving the senses of sight and sound. The skilled interviewer is aware of the subtleties and shades of meaning that can be communicated, and is sensitive to the differences which age, social environment and intellectual ability can introduce. For examples of good and bad communication see the chapter of *Reflections on Recruitment* pages 47–90).

To a degree which is often underestimated, the interview may impose 'threats' and pressures on the candidate's personality make-up. Status, occupational competence and personal affairs are being exposed to scrutiny. The candidate's livelihood and even the hopes and aspirations of her or his family may rest upon the outcome and the interviewee will naturally be anxious to present him/herself in a favourable light. However, there is a problem. Voluntary disclosure of information may seem like a betrayal of confidences; but non-disclosure may land him or her in a job which he or she cannot do or does not want to do. The skilled interviewer will be sensitive to such pressures. Throughout, the interview will be handled with a delicate touch, giving reassurance after threat and offering the candidates an opportunity present themselves in their best light before uncovering weaknesses.

Bias, prejudice and 'halo effect'

Interviewers can be their own worst enemies. Their efforts towards objectivity will founder if they allow prejudice or bias to distort their judgements. Almost everyone has some prejudices. Though the interviewer will not rid themselves of them completely, they should strive to be aware of them.

Bias and prejudice result partly from the cultural and environmental influences within which a person has been brought up and partly from the way in which we as individuals have reacted to those background influences. Inevitably, interviewers' own attitudes towards work and towards society reflect their own background to a greater or lesser extent. In order to judge fairly what kind of a person the candidate really is, the interviewer needs to discount personal likes and dislikes and to examine impartially that other person's background and attitudes. Frequently, it will be found that the candidate's background and that of the interviewer have certain features in common, and this can lead to bias on the part of the interviewer; conversely, if the candidate's reactions run counter to the interviewer's, he or she may be biased against that particular candidate. Judgement can be warped in this way without the interviewer being conscious of it.

Prejudices, on the other hand, tend to be associated with persistent attitudes held by the interviewer. Commonly, they are directed towards personal characteristics possessed by other people. Examples are prejudice against people with certain facial features, such as low forehead or a receding chin; against some regional accent, a personal mannerism or aspect of dress; or against those of another race, colour or creed. Such irrational notions are inimical to good interviewing. Though the interviewer may find it impossible to discard prejudices there should be an awareness of their existence and allowance should be made for them in any final assessment. The great danger in bias and prejudice is that they lead to unfair discrimination. Much has been said and written about various forms of discrimination; sexual, racial and colour discrimination can now be challenged at industrial tribunals and penalties will be awarded for infringement. Positive discrimination against the trend is sometimes tolerated, e.g. in favour of an ethnic minority, and one suspects that a few organizations have swung too far in the other extreme to avoid the stigma of such a charge. The fact remains, however, that most of us nurse attitudes, often subliminally, which are hard to eradicate until they are exposed for what they are. For example, in preparing the original version of this text in 1968 'he' was used throughout without any thought as to the bias it proclaimed which was entirely cultural. The career woman was then largely unknown in industry outside certain functions such as personnel, medicine, and administration. Times have now changed and the career woman is the rule rather than the exception – though women are still poorly represented in senior management. The same is true of certain ethnic minorities – especially those we term 'coloured'. The individual charged with the task of recruitment is in the front line and needs to be very aware of 'unfair discrimination' and consciously seek to avoid it. Whilst one should not exaggerate and whilst objective and factually based evaluations are acceptable, the question should be asked of all selection criteria; is this criterion socially just? Is this question or test unfairly loaded? Why do we think that a woman, an older man, an African national or someone with strong political views should be automatically excluded? The personnel department is the keeper of the organization's conscience in conforming to the law and in addition to this it should be responsible for recruiting the best people available. Many of these have been quite unfairly, and foolishly, rejected in the past for totally illogical and indefensible reasons such as sex, age, colour or creed.

A more subtle source of error is know as '*the halo effect*'. This occurs when the interviewer, having been impressed favourably (or unfavourably) by one attribute of the candidate, allows any judgement of the candidate's other attributes to be swamped and assigns to them correspondingly high (or low) ratings. Thus an interviewer confronted, for example, by a candidate whose appearance and bearing seem to be ideal for that job may give her credit for more experience or intelligence than she really possesses. If most of the other applicants for the job have already been eliminated, the interviewer may be especially prone to this form of 'halo effect'.

Note-taking

Uncertainty about when, where and how to take notes during an interview seems to be a common source of difficulty to those with limited experience. Some note-taking is usually necessary, especially by the inexperienced interviewer. This is particularly true when several candidates are to be seen in sequence and the time between interviews is short.

The approach to note-taking must vary according to the interviewer's powers of concentration and the reliability of her or his memory. Both faculties can be cultivated to a high degree by systematic training, but the untrained memory is notoriously selective and fickle. The interviewer must develop the ability to recall accurately what has been said during the past hour or so. This calls for no superhuman effort; it is a requirement of the job. Ability to do this is taken for granted in other spheres. All professional actors accept that they must memorize vast quantities of dialogue, actions and movements. Likewise, professional interviewers will minimize their dependence on written notes, and will need only a few 'prompts' to revive their memory of an interview. The following points are helpful as a practical guide:

(a) Always ask the candidate's permission before taking notes. Few refuse and, indeed, many seem pleased by the implication that what they are saying is important enough to be recorded.

(b) Never take notes furtively. Write quite openly, but in such a position that the candidate is unable to read what is written.

(c) Take a minimum of notes and confine them to 'memory triggers' and important facts not recorded elsewhere. They should serve as *aide-memoires* and not as a verbatim recording.

(d) Never let note-taking interrupt the flow of conversation.

(e) Be careful about timing. Highly personal or adverse information should not be noted until the conversation has moved to a different topic.

Number of interviewers

For the great bulk of recruitment work the one-to-one type of interview (i.e. one interviewer with one candidate) is most frequently used. Even so, the candidate will often have more than one interview before being offered an appointment, the preliminary screening being conducted by a member of the personnel department and the subsequent interview by the head of the department concerned. For certain types of appointment, there can be advantages in having more than one interviewer present but it must be remembered that this will produce a very different reaction in the mind of the candidate.

The one-to-one situation is generally preferred, because rapport is established more easily and it allows the interviewer to be more flexible in approach and in the framing and timing of follow-up questions. Candidates respond more naturally and freely in the informal atmosphere of this setting. It also makes less heavy demands on management time, since the second interviewer sees only those applicants who have survived the preliminary interview. Conversely, more of the candidate's time is taken up by a sequence of interviews and, if these cannot be held on the same day, there may be a risk that the most able applicant will be offered and accept a job elsewhere.

Some authorities recommend that two interviewers should see the candidate simultaneously and claim that this method reduces bias and subjectivity. Two interviewers can be useful in situations when a large number of applicants must be seen in a short period of time, and when one of the interviewers is a technical expert. Even so, it is important that the interviewers should have agreed beforehand the role which each is to play. Usually, one conducts the greater part of the interview, whilst the other observes and makes notes until being invited to pose specialist or supplementary questions towards the end of the discussion. This type of interview situation does, of course, have value in the training of new interviewers.

Panel interviews are favoured by some writers. The panel usually comprises three to five assessors. Its principal value is at the final short list stage for some senior appointments, when several departments need to be identified with the eventual appointment. Advantages claimed for the panel interview are that it reduces bias and subjectivity; ensures that an expert on each topic asks the questions; enables user and other departments to be represented; increases impressiveness and formality; sets up uniform standards of judgement; and requires candidates to explain themselves only once. But, unless all the assessors are highly trained and adhere to their allotted roles, most of these potential advantages will be lost. In the governmental, educational or local authority ambience, where they are widely used, its weaknesses are that one interviewer with a strong personality can dominate the others; members of the panel may tend to show off to impress each other; formality reduces flexibility and inhibits the establishment of rapport; some candidates may be overawed or reluctant to talk freely on personal matters; only the formal behaviour of the candidate is observed; the smooth flow of conversation is obstructed and the pattern of questioning can become haphazard unless it is firmly controlled.

Selection boards comprising more than five assessors are rarely used as a serious selection device in industry. Insofar as they appear to exist, they are often little more than a convenient vehicle for introducing the final candidate(s) to a full committee; in many cases, the effective choice will already have been made by a sub-committee or by a permanent official whose recommendation is being submitted for ratification.

Interpreting the interview

By the end of the interview, the candidate and the interviewer will each have accumulated facts and impressions which they did not have before. Each is faced with the task of digesting and interpreting this new information. The interview is a two-way affair. Information flows in both directions and a separate assessment is made by each party. If the interview has been conducted properly the candidate will have a fairly detailed picture of the company, the job, co-workers, and the conditions of employment. Some of the more important gaps will have been filled in by observation and by asking questions during the course of the interview. Impressions will have been formed about the interviewer (who personifies the company for the candidate) and also about the way in which information has been given or withheld. On such evidence a decision will be made as to whether or not to accept the job if it were to be offered.

For her part, the interviewer will have learned much from the candidate's questions, as well as from her own. She will have noted the type and depth of the questions, the candidate's grasp of the information given to him, the quality of his reasoning and his verbal ability. These clues will be stored in the interviewer's mind, together with all the other evidence acquired during the selection process which she must now marshall and analyse. The framework she uses is the person specification (described in chapter 1). Throughout the interview she will have borne in mind the essential and desirable attributes demanded by the job and particularly any contra-indications which may have been specified. Her task now is to judge how closely the candidate meets those requirements.

In some cases, the interviewer will already have concluded on factual grounds that the candidate is unsuitable for the job by failing to meet one of the essential requirements. Even so, a fairly full assessment should be recorded so that the candidate may be considered in relation to other vacancies which could arise in the future. More often, the interviewer has to judge the degree to which the candidate possesses the desired attributes. This is done by considering all the clues picked up at various points throughout the interview. Evidence about the candidate's interests, for example, may have emerged when discussing family circumstances, school hobbies, attitude to overtime work etc, and the interviewer must piece this information together in order to discern the underlying pattern. One practical method of doing so is to:

- assemble the facts of the candidate's career in chronological order;
- superimpose the candidate's explanations and attitudes using quotations of the candidate's actual words when possible;
- examine the trends and behaviour patterns;
- consider the candidate's progress and rate of development in relation to peers. Compared with people from a similar background and with similar opportunities, has her/his progress been below average, about average or better than average?

Whilst the interview is in progress and afterwards, the interviewer will formulate working hypotheses about the candidate and then search for evidence in past and present behaviour to confirm or refute those hypotheses. A useful technique is to visualize the candidate at work in typical situations and to consider how she might behave. ('I can see her coping convincingly with even our toughest customers . . . ').

The interviewer aims to build up a coherent picture of the salient features of the candidate's life. Only a few bare bones had previously been apparent from the candidate's own written statements. Flesh is added by piecing together all the further information gleaned from the interview. This process of reconstruction and appraisal is a vitally important one. By taking into account what the candidate has already achieved and why he has done so, the interviewer is better equipped to judge how that candidate would be likely to perform if faced with the demands inherent in the job for which he has applied.

Information sessions

A new technique which the author has been developing is that of a formal 'information session'. This can be group or individual and is especially appropriate at senior levels or when a project team is being assembled or where the competition is open, e.g. public appointments. Candidates are given a full brief beforehand and encouraged to do their own search about the company and its executive team. This may be supplemented by a formal audio/visual presentation at the short list stage at the beginning of the day. Candidates are then invited to ask questions and to make observations. In effect there is a reversal of roles with the candidate in charge of the seminar. This technique has been used in two ways:

(a) potential colleague – candidates for a board appointment have met other directors/departmental heads either as a group (preferably) or individually. Insight, judgement, tact, interpersonal sensitivity and management style are quickly revealed.

(b) potential superior – the candidates (individually) spend a set time (40 mins) with two to three future key subordinates seeking both information and to set a basis for a future working relationship. Quality of questioning and handling of the session are recorded by observers supplemented later on by comments from the 'interviewees'.

In both cases the seminars are timed and observed by trained observers with a written brief and ratings are made.

On the whole the reaction of candidates has been very favourable although the seminar, run in an informal atmosphere, is demanding – and revealing. The 'interviewees' must be carefully briefed not to take over the session and to keep to the point in their answers.

Group selection methods

Summary

Among the qualities which neither the interview nor intelligence tests are able to assess accurately are the candidate's ability to get on with and influence future colleagues, to display qualities of spontaneous leadership and to produce ideas in a real life situation. To meet this need, group selection procedures have been evolved. They usually take the form of a group exercise centred on a real or imaginary problem. Developed by the German army before the 1939–45 war, they have since been used extensively for officer selection in HM Forces, by the Civil Service Commission, and for assessment prior to management training courses by some industrial concerns. Given adequate safeguards they can be used with success also in the selection of executives.

Group procedures are not used as widely as might be expected for several reasons, perhaps the chief ones being the difficulty of recording and interpreting the information, the time taken and the unwillingness of some candidates to participate in a face to face competitive situation.

Purpose

Group procedures provide evidence about candidates' abilities to:

- get on with others;
- influence others, and their manner of doing so;
- express themselves in verbal terms;
- think clearly and logically;
- argue from past experience and apply knowledge, intelligence and experience to a new problem.

They also reveal the types of social role they tend to play.

These characteristics break down into two major parts: intellectual skills and social skills. In addition, other personality factors are displayed and these may substantiate impressions gained during the interview, such as the existence of strongly held attitudes, likes and dislikes.

Procedures

Three main types of situation or exercise can be used. These are:

(a) Leaderless groups (usually discussion)
(b) Command or executive exercises
(c) Group problem-solving.

(a) Leaderless groups
About six to eight candidates are given a topic of general interest to discuss: or they may be asked to choose their topic. The setting has to be arranged carefully, so that no one chair dominates the rest. As with all groups, the members should be of comparable standing. The discussion is timed strictly, using a stop-watch, and everything is recorded and observed by a number of assessors placed inconspicuously in the corners of the room. The group do not know the topic for discussion until they have been briefed. ('We should like to hear your views on this topic. We want you all to take part, even if you feel you cannot contribute much to the discussion by way of experience: you may well have more experience to call on than you realize. You will have exactly . . . minutes. Tackle the subject in whatever way you feel to be most suitable. You may now start as soon as you are ready.')

Using a system of recording *who-said-what-to-whom*, the observers assess the type and quality of each member's contribution and the reaction of the others to it. At the end of the discussion, the group are thanked and given a break, while the assessors consider and compare their rankings.

The encouraging – and perhaps surprising – point about the leaderless discussion group, is that each member tends to play a similar role on each occasion, provided that the topic is a controversial one of general interest.

(b) Command or executive situation
The candidates are given an extensive brief, based on a real life situation. In executive selection this might be the description and history of a company, including its leading personalities and current problems. The brief then leads to a typical job problem. The candidates are given the brief on the previous day, and have time to study it. Executive roles are allocated. On the following day,

each in turn takes the chair, outlines a solution to one of the problems and defends it before the rest of the committee. Sometimes a composite problem is used, where each will take an extended role throughout the whole period.

Again, the members are observed throughout and rankings are compared.

(c) Group problem-solving

This is a combination of the other two. The group is leaderless and is usually described as an advisory committee: how it organizes itself is left to the group to decide. The problem is often relevant to the job which is to be filled. It should be preferably beyond the experience of any individual in the group, but one to which each member can contribute according to knowledge, experience and intellectual skill. The problem is generally a large one, so that pressure is imposed to solve it within the given time.

Members of the group are carefully briefed and timed. As with other group selection methods, their behaviour is observed and recorded, but in assessing individual contributions previous experience is taken into account.

Interpretation

Social skills: Each candidate is ranked on social skill and the role taken (or attempted). Social skill includes sensitivity to others, tact, aggressiveness, hostility, friendliness, withdrawal, reaction when contradicted or criticized; how the candidate saves face or modifies his or her views. Social role takes account of the extent to which others listen to, ignore, shout down or become hostile to him or her; whether he/she becomes accepted as chairperson, expert, group coordinator, ideas person etc. The way the candidate attempts to influence others, the way others are handled and the amount of respect engendered will be the major things looked for.

Intellectual skills: The quality and quantity of the candidate's contributions are analysed for clarity of thought e.g. ability to express ideas logically and forcibly; the quality of analogies and generalizations; ability to apply both knowledge and experience to the problem; flexibility of thinking and the weight carried in argument or discussion. Ratings are generally given of general intelligence displayed; quality of argument; influence in argument; and ability in applying knowledge and experience.

Strong attitudes: These are often provoked in discussion but difficult to detect during an interview. The staunch authoritarian, the 'leaf in the wind', the fairminded, the 'one solution, one problem' people all come to the surface at some time or other. Strong political, racial or religious attitudes may often be revealed.

Self or 'buddy' ratings: After the discussion, candidates are sometimes asked to assess the contribution of the other members and to express their likes and dislikes of them. Sometimes they may be reluctant to do so, but generally this can be achieved, and sociograms compiled of the results.

Difficulties implicit in group selection − when to use and when not to use:

Group exercises are time-consuming and therefore costly. They are appropriate only for appointments where social leadership skills are required; hence they can be used for supervisory and management appointments and, at the final short list stage, can be a convenient means of seeing all the candidates on one day.

They are less likely to be successful when used with under 18s, and even then should be reserved for the A Level group. The younger ones are unlikely to contribute much and, in any case, may not take the procedure sufficiently seriously. Their experience is limited and their ideas are still in the formative stage. Likewise group procedures are unlikely to be particularly successful with people who are not very articulate or who are not used to solving problems by means of words. In theory it would of course be possible for a group of manual workers to solve a design problem by the use of hand and machine tools and materials. One would not normally need to test such ingenuity in this way. To aid the less articulate it is possible to produce a series of documents of a type with which they will be familiar so that they have the basic problem solving material in their hands. At one time, following the use of group selection and assessment procedures for the selection of officers during the war, they became a favourite tool with ex-service industrial managements for the selection of future management trainees. Hence they tend to be used for the selection of the more articulate school leavers, for graduates and for others who want to join management training courses. They have been used over the years by firms of consultants in the selection of senior management, but they are not a popular device among senior, experienced candidates from outside a company.

Today group selection procedures (outside the civil service) tend to be used much more for in-company selections to supervisory or to managerial posts. Although candidates are in direct competition and may know one another, there is a feeling that this is a much fairer way of selecting people. All are set the same task to perform and are judged on their work performance rather than, say, on their past record. Group selection procedures can be as successful in selecting future supervisors as in selecting future general management.

Assessment centres

This concept has been growing in popularity: groups of employees are put through a series of tests and group exercises at an assessment centre, which is equipped to administer such tests and with company personnel trained in the interpretation of test results.

Composition of the group is important and there should be about six to eight participants. They should all be of similar ages and have roughly the same level of experience. A mixed group of men and women is generally to be avoided except at more senior levels. Until society as a whole has accepted full equality among the sexes, male dominance or the tendency to impress the other sex will destroy the value of the session by uncontrollable distortion. Choice of topic is also important and should be decided by a psychologist or trained layperson.

A major drawback in using group selection techniques as part of a normal recruitment procedure, particularly with older and more experienced candidates, is that the identity of each candidate becomes known to the others. This can be a serious consideration when the field to choose from is small, or candidates are drawn from competing companies. The acceptability of the selection procedure can stand or fall by this criterion alone, which should always be carefully weighed in advance. Very broadly, group selection methods are acceptable to the under 40s, and to aspiring executives if the field of candidates is reasonably wide.

The personnel manager who may be contemplating using group exercises for the first time is advised to become thoroughly acquainted with the relevant literature. A course of training in the principles, and some practice in their interpretation, is highly desirable.

Psychological tests

Summary

Properly administered and interpreted, psychometric tests are the most reliable instrument in the personnel assessor's tool kit. They are designed to measure 'brain power' (i.e. problem-solving ability), special aptitudes (e.g. the ability to think in three dimensions, the ability to use past experience to tackle new problems) and levels of skill (e.g. vocabulary) and to analyse personality make-up. Tests can be given individually or formed into batteries. Interpretation is by reference to statistically derived tables which compare performance with that of groups such as university graduates, printing trainees, medical practitioners, pilots etc. Practical 'job sample' tests can be used to assess manual dexterity, colour vision, secretarial or managerial skills. Personality tests are more problematic; they are less reliable (people change) and more difficult to measure. However, certain tests are widely used and are better than guess work. Interpretation is the principal difficulty. This is best left to the professional psychologist. 'Short-cut' tests marketed widely should be viewed with caution and advice sought before applying them. Other methods such as graphology, astrology, colour preferences need to be viewed with even more caution and left to the professionals (psychologists are unlikely to use them). They are nonetheless popular outside the UK (graphology is practised widely in France and Germany).

Using selection tests is not a new idea. Examples can be found in ancient literature and throughout history.[1] However, the introduction of psychological tests into industry has been fraught with

[1] Two selection tests were used by Gideon in choosing 300 men from his army of 32,000 to fight the Philistines. See *Old Testament*, Judges VII, vv 1–7.

suspicion and misunderstanding. Controversy persists in spite of abundant evidence that certain tests, properly used, have high predictive value in the occupational sphere. They are being employed on an increasing scale in the UK, but not as yet to the same extent as in the United States. Selectors and candidates are likely to feel strongly about tests; and a number of popular books have been published on the subject, in addition to the considerable scientific literature. Emotion can run so high that the value and limitations of tests fail to be seen in a true perspective. In recent years many tests have had to be very carefully pruned to ensure that they are genuinely 'culture fair' and eliminate social, racial or sexual bias. This is no mean task; some aspects can pose very serious technical problems to the test constructor especially if the test is to be applied to newcomers to a country or those brought up within exclusive communities within the host country.

Test scores should never be used as the sole criterion in making an appointment. Tests do not supplant the interview but, in appropriate cases, they can supplement and strengthen it. The interview has too many advantages to be discarded. Quite apart from its technical value as an assessment technique, it serves as a flexible and convenient framework for a face to face meeting and has the intrinsic merit of enabling questions about the job to be raised and answered. Tests can, however, measure some attributes which are difficult to assess by interview. They can thus help to reduce the areas of subjective judgement and of possible human error in the selection process as a whole. A word of warning is necessary: tests in the hands of an untrained person can be more misleading than helpful. That is not to say that only the qualified psychologist can make use of tests (though this does apply to some of them). However, the inexperienced person does need a formal course of training in how to apply and interpret those tests which are available for use. This chapter summarizes the main types of tests which are of potential interest to the practising personnel officer and indicates the circumstances in which they may be helpful. It also suggests that either a formal training course in psychological testing should be taken or the interviewer should refrain from dabbling with such tests.

Main types of tests

The tests in current use fall into five main categories, each of which is briefly described below:

(a) General intelligence (or general aptitude)
(b) Special aptitude (loosely referred to as 'aptitude')
(c) Attainment
(d) Typical performance
(e) Personality

(a) General intelligence tests

Intelligence is one of the hardest things to assess accurately from interview evidence alone. Verbal fluency can easily be mistaken for high intelligence and, conversely, hesitancy in speech may be confused with low intelligence. The candidate with an indifferent scholastic record may possess considerable innate ability which was not fully tapped during school days. Tests of general intelligence can help to provide a factual baseline. Before describing intelligence tests, it is necessary to consider what is actually meant by 'intelligence'.

Controversy persists in academic circles about the precise definition of 'intelligence'. The subtleties of the arguments need not concern us here, since most psychologists are broadly agreed about what the term conveys. In lay language, intelligence tests are simply a means of measuring performance on a standard series of mental tasks; and they are important because it can be shown statistically that a person's ability to score highly on such tasks correlates with the capacity to learn and retain new knowledge, to pass examinations and to succeed at work. The fact that a person has the necessary mental capacity does not, by itself, guarantee success at work; but if that capacity is lacking, success will never be attained however hard he or she may try.

Vincent[1] postulates three forms of intelligence: *innate intelligence*, i.e. a person's capacity to perform on a standard series of mental tasks; *effective intelligence*, i.e. the extent to which that capacity is used in real life situations; and *practical intelligence*, i.e. worldly wisdom or the ability to learn from experience and

[1] Vincent, D. F. *Age and Test Performance*, National Institute of Industrial Psychology, Occasional Paper.

apply that knowledge to new situations. Vincent suggests that 'innate intelligence and effective intelligence are closely related. Although effective intelligence will vary with the occasion, persons of high innate intelligence will on average display high effective intelligence. The undoubted value of intelligence tests, that is, of measures of innate intelligence, is partly due to this relationship and partly to the fact that in the situations for which they are used to predict success, such as passing an examination or doing some responsible work, people usually do use their wits and their average effective intelligence is not usually lower than their innate intelligence. If the situation is one of importance, a person's effective intelligence is not likely to be much lower than the innate intelligence, but the efficiency with which the situation is handled, his/her practical intelligence, will depend upon innate intelligence plus knowledge plus experience.'

Practical intelligence can be measured by tests such as Watson Glaser Critical Thinking Appraisal and is also shown by the quality of reasoning displayed at interview and during group exercises. The term 'street-wise' refers, in part, to such abilities.

Before using any test, the personnel officer must ensure that it measures accurately and reliably what it is supposed to measure. It must also be established that what the test measures is a significant factor in occupational success.

Most tests of general aptitude and of special aptitude contain a common factor (referred to as 'g') which is postulated as 'general intelligence'. This common factor is present to a greater degree in some tests than in others. A person with high general intelligence will do well, therefore, on all such tests, but performance may vary from one test to another according to the extent to which each test measures other special abilities as well. (The latter can be isolated or set in relief by tests of special aptitude.) Individual people are able to apply their general intelligence better to certain types of material than to others. Thus, some will respond best to verbal or language-based tests; others to a sequence of patterns and spatial designs; and others to tests based on numerical series. In order to arrive at an accurate measure of a person's general intelligence, it is necessary to use both a verbal test and a non-verbal one. The verbal (or v:ed) test reflects in known quantity a person's previous education; hence, when considered in relation to the amount of education already received, it may provide clues to ability to benefit further from verbally-based education or training.

(b) Special aptitude tests

Individual people differ greatly in their psychological make-up. Some possess a distinct flair for languages, for example, whilst others are more at home with mechanical things. Tests have been devised to measure certain of these special aptitudes such as mechanical ability (including electrical and other engineering types of activity); clerical; numerical; spatial; and, to a lesser extent, artistic and creative capacities. These special aptitude tests are generally incorporated in test batteries, which also include tests of attainment and of general intelligence. As indicated above, a person with high general intelligence will score well on most of these tests depending on their 'g' content or loading. Special aptitudes can be discerned by comparing performance on the general and the special aptitude tests. Interpretive tables (or norms) have been devised on an occupational basis for some test batteries, thus enabling individual scores to be compared with these norms when selecting engineering apprentices, printing apprentices, trainee accountants, secretaries, computer programmers, clerical workers etc.

Manual dexterity is particularly hard to isolate, since it seems to take many different forms according to the degree of spatial judgement and coordination involved and the relative movements of the fingers, hands, wrists and arms. No single test suffices for all permutations of manual dexterity, but many specific tests have been devised by psychologists to suit the particular demands of various jobs. These often take the form of timed runs on work samples. For semi-skilled jobs, quite a number of such tests have been devised and shown to be successul.

(c) Tests of attainment

Attainment tests seek to measure a person's range and depth of knowledge of a subject and grasp of its basic principles. Since the marking of such tests involves no subjective interpretation, they provide an accurate guide to a person's current knowledge and highlight strengths and weaknesses within that subject. With some job applicants, they can be a better indicator of current knowledge than school examination results, particularly if those examinations were taken some years ago; or if the candidate has a good short term memory without a proper grasp of the basic principles; or if the particular questions in the examination papers called on only a small sample of knowledge.

Although the unqualified can devise attainment tests they are ill-advised to do so, unless they have a thorough understanding of the statistical concepts involved. For example, a battery of attainment tests for secretarial work will cover vocabulary, grammar, spelling, punctuation, arithmetic etc, and within each aspect the items will be graded in order of difficulty, so that the battery will show the candidate's level of attainment and degree of accuracy.

(d) Test of typical performance
This category of test is self-explanatory. Examples are shorthand and typing tests, with the items well graded in order of difficulty.

(e) Personality tests
Originally designed as diagnostic aids to clinical and psychiatric medicine, several types of personality test have been used successfully by members of the medical profession for many years. When transplanted to the industrial scene, personality tests become the most controversial of all psychological tests. Of course it would be tremendously helpful in industrial selection work if the interview evidence could always be supported by personality tests, of proven validity and reliability, which were acceptable in the normal course of assessing candidates. Unfortunately, that stage has not yet been reached. Much research is still needed. Some recent tests show promise but need considerable skill in interpretation. The personnel officer who is contemplating using any personality tests would be prudent to obtain professional advice before doing so; and the serious reservations held by many leading psychologists should be borne in mind.

Other types of test have been developed and tried commercially with apparent success (i.e. the results are significantly better than chance). However, psychologists remain sceptical: objective measurement is often impossible to achieve in experiment and so much depends on the author's powers of interpretation. This includes tests based on graphology (handwriting analysis), astrology, colour preferences, palmistry, phrenology or a study of bodily postures and movements. As with many tests developed in war-time to test the reaction of troops under battle stress, pencil and paper tests produce consistently as good if not better results, are measurable and do not depend entirely on the interpreter. Graphology is particularly favoured in France and in Germany. (The author has tested candidates using AH4 and 16PF and a graphologist has done likewise. Whilst there was some convergence and no significant contra-indications more could be learned from the AH4/16PF combination with the back-up of stastistical probability. Further research in this area could be useful.)

When to use tests

Since tests, like the interview, are a means of eliciting information about the candidate, much depends on what is already known about him or her and what it is necessary to find out or to confirm. The older the candidate, the more should be apparent already from the 'track record', provided that a good application form is being used. Hence, the marginal value of tests diminishes with age and, as a general guide, tests are not usually given to candidates over 40, except in special circumstances.

Acceptability is an important consideration. Tests can be made much more acceptable than is sometimes supposed, provided they are introduced carefully and explained properly. Sixth formers and university leavers will take them without demur; aspiring executives under 30 will appreciate their relevance; ageing workers, transferring to other jobs, will accept them as inevitable; some executives over 40 may react unfavourably since the threat is greater, especially for successful people who have worked their way up from the bottom; and for executives over 50 tests are rarely of great value, since the peak of development will have been reached and practical intelligence is more relevant.

The appropriateness of testing will therefore vary according to the type and level of the various jobs to be filled. It is desirable for a company to give clear policy guidance on the range of jobs, if any, for which tests should be used as part of the standard selection procedures. In this way, the company will be able to compile its own test norms over a period, in relation to those categories of jobs. A number of test agencies and consultancies have been established which use specially validated test batteries which they have developed for specific clients and which are regularly applied and researched. Some large organizations have this as an internal service. Companies, or departments, refer individuals to them for an 'in depth' assessment, usually at the short list stage or when they want to promote from within. Other individuals can be referred to these and other psychologists for assessment against their management or functional norms which are often tentative, and therefore unpublished, but which nevertheless have a potentially high predictive value.

Tests can be particularly useful when:

Recruiting school leavers: The factual information obtainable from tests is especially valuable when selecting for apprenticeships and for other long courses of training. Some firms give general intelligence tests to all school leavers, and special aptitude batteries to the more promising ones. When interpreted in conjunction with a professional vocational guidance interview, tests can assist remarkably in launching school leavers on a suitable vocation at the right level.

Assessing 'trainability': With more mature applicants, too, tests can be helpful in selecting those most likely to respond to training. A battery of general intelligence, special aptitude and attainment tests is most commonly used to measure capacity and 'trainability'.

Assessing for promotion or transfer: Not all good skilled workers have the capacity to become good supervisors, nor all sales representatives to become sales managers. Nor for that matter do good line managers necessarily make good general managers. On promotion other skills will be needed; in many cases skills analysis has shown that frequently new managers have to learn virtually entirely new jobs, since for 75 per cent or more of their time they will need to use an entirely new range of skills. Rosemary Stewart and her team at the Oxford Centre for Management Studies have done some interesting work in this area. Research experiments have shown a positive correlation between intelligence (especially verbal intelligence) and managerial potential. Given an employee's academic and career record plus a measure of innate capacity, a reasonably accurate prediction can be made of ceiling for promotion. Similarly, when considering the possible transfer of an ageing skilled worker to office work, a clerical battery can indicate whether the employee's abilities lie in that direction.

A further situation is where major change is to be introduced following, for example, a change in management style or mode of working as a result of a takeover or merger. Tests can remove a lot of the guesswork and provide objective, unbiased evaluations and reveal ability to respond to retraining and adapt to change or fit into a new cultural structure.

How to use tests

It is essential to adhere strictly to the testing conditions laid down in the manual supplied with the tests. Applicants must be introduced to the test situation with extreme care. If the selector explains why the tests are being used, suspicion will be allayed and resistance will diminish. Tests should be given when the candidates are mentally fresh and they should therefore form an early part of the selection procedure.

Many tests have an initial practice section, which is not scored, to ensure that all candidates are familiar with what is expected of them. They also serve another purpose. Coaching in test methods, like coaching in school examination methods, can enhance an individual's performance marginally. Doing similar tests several times can also produce a marginal improvement. The practice sections serve to reduce these effects. Some publishers supply parallel tests of equivalent difficulty as a means of overcoming the effects of coaching and practice.

Test scores are usually interpreted by referring to tables of norms. These enable the candidate's performance to be compared with the known performances of hundreds, and sometimes thousands, of other people of similar age and education. Thus each candidate can be ranked in relation to a much larger population than lies within the personal experience of the assessor. Validity researches showing correlations between test performance and later academic or occupational success are also available, so it is possible to assess the statistical probability of the candidate reaching the required level of attainment. On some types of test (but not all) there is a predictable decline in performance as age increases, and age adjustment tables are supplied.

In recruitment work there are three distinct stages in interpreting the candidate's test performance in order to predict suitability:

(i) actual scores are related to the appropriate norms tables;
(ii) test performance is compared with career record;
(iii) the latter are related to the requirements of the job.

There are divided views on whether the test results should be made available to the interviewer before or after seeing the candidate. Some interviewers feel that they might be over influenced by knowing the test results in advance; and others feel that the test results help them to pitch the interview at the right level and to seek explanations for apparent inconsistencies. There is no absolute rule. Much depends on the style and professional competence of the interviewer.

Points of reference

Summary

It is often necessary to check facts and statements made in application forms and at interview. Research has shown that many candidates 'stretch the truth'. References can also give reassurance and help to paint a fuller picture of the candidates. Written references have to be read with caution; why were they written, by whom and what has been left out? They do have a place, however, and can be a useful confirmation of facts such as qualifications, dates of joining and leaving, reasons for leaving, exact job titles etc. Verbal references are also useful but must be used with care and discretion. A verbal reference is a 'privileged character' in law but must not be knowingly false or discreditable. Good referencing needs care and preparation. The referee needs to know why it is wanted and what kind of information is sought. Confidentiality is vital.

It is common practice for an offer of appointment to be made 'subject to satisfactory references'. This escape clause is often inserted even though the employer may not bother to take up references or may consider it unnecessary to do so. It is easy to fall into the trap of regarding references as a procedural appendage which comes after the effective decision to engage an applicant has already been made. This attitude of mind can cause the selector to overlook sources of information which may be very important indeed. Properly conceived, references are an integral part of the assessment process.

Towards the latter stage of the selection process, the assessor has learnt a good deal about the candidate. But inevitably that knowledge is based on only a small sample of the candidate's total experience and behaviour. Moreover, much of it has been derived in the formalized contexts of application forms, psychological tests, interviews etc. These contexts are not, and cannot be, typical of the conditions under which the candidate normally works or will be required to work if engaged. Before reaching a final assessment the personnel officer must ask how much of this information consists of established facts about the candidate and how much is made up of impressions and unsubstantiated claims. From this a decision must be made on what else is needed to find out or confirm. Some of these gaps in knowledge can be filled by seeking 'references', in the widest sense of that term.

It is true that a reference usually cannot, and should not, be obtained from the candidate's present employer, until an offer of engagement is being made; even then, no approach should be made unless and until the candidate's explicit agreement has been obtained. But that is only one source of relevant information. Other sources are available and can be used without risk of embarrassment to the candidate.

(a) School record
When assessing school leavers or juveniles already employed, confirmation of scholastic achievements can be obtained from the headmaster or youth employment officer. Head teachers can often predict fairly accurately students' chances of passing academic examinations for which they are still studying, and for examinations where academic standards are known such as a university degree. Some employers are prone to assume that head teachers can also predict a student's suitability to join their company. Clearly, it is unreasonable to expect this, unless the employer has first taken the trouble to give a clear understanding of the particular type of job or apprenticeship for which the girl or boy is being considered. Heads and careers teachers will also give you useful

comparative data such as how well a pupil mixes at school, interest in out of curriculum activities, and the amount of leadership displayed and responsibility taken while at school. It is not then difficult to translate this type of information to the industrial or commercial environment. On the whole the reports of handicrafts or art teachers are rarely useful, as standards set at school are so far below those expected in industry. Indeed, I have known a so-called prowess of young people in such subjects as geometrical drawing at school to bear an inverse relationship to their later skill on the drawing board.

(b) Professional qualifications and university degrees
Confirmation is readily obtainable. A printed form or model letter is a useful and acceptable method of requesting this confirmation. It should always show the candidate's full name and the exact dates on which the relevant examinations are claimed to have been passed.

Many professional bodies publish year books which list the names of their members. Reference to up-to-date year books can save time, when large scale recruitment of professionally qualified staff is being undertaken. They need to be interpreted with care, since the absence of the candidate's name may be due to nothing more sinister than a printer's omission or the fact that a subscription has lapsed.

(c) Open testimonials
No hard and fast rules about written testimonials can be laid down. Much depends upon what is said and who says it. Some firms prefer to give testimonials to employees who are leaving, in order to save the time that might otherwise be taken up in answering subsequent requests for references from prospective employers. If testimonials are couched in factual and explicit terms, they should not be dismissed out of hand. Many are openly addressed 'To whom it may concern', precisely because the employer is well-satisfied with an employee's work and wants to show that this is the case. Even so, they are often too generalized to be of much value. For example:

This is to certify that John Brown is an honest and conscientious worker. During his period of employment here, he has been

given a variety of jobs to do and has tackled them to the utmost
of his ability. We wish him well in his future carreer.

Not surprisingly, this type of testimonial (often produced during
the course of an interview) is read solemnly, and then quietly
disregarded. It conveys virtually nothing of value. On the other
hand, the example below (*if true!*) would convey a good deal of
worthwhile information about the same person:

I hereby certify that John Brown has been employed at this
garage since 1981. He is a thoroughly reliable and conscientious
mechanic. In the course of his work here, he has undertaken
major overhauls and minor repairs on many different types of
cars, motor cycles and lorries, including diesel-engined vehicles.
Although he did not serve an apprenticeship, he can be relied
upon to carry out repair and maintenance work to a high stan-
dard, and without supervision. He gets on well with customers
and workmates, and has always shown himself to be a man of
sober and temperate habits. We are sorry that he has decided
to leave us but recognize that we cannot offer him the early
advancement which he merits.

(d) Closed references
Other people's assessments of the candidate's character or
employment history can be taken into account more systematically
by asking them for references. Their value will depend on how
well the referee knows the candidate and on the exact wording of
the questions asked. A reference is a privileged document, and
that privilege must not be abused; all statements must be true or
honestly believed to be true by their author. The more factual
the reference, the easier it is to substantiate, the easier it is to
convey and the easier it is to interpret. Employers are more willing
than is sometimes supposed to supply confidential and factual
answers to questions about a former employee's length of service,
duties, rate of pay, reasons for leaving etc.

The method of obtaining references will vary according to the
type and level of the job to be filled. Generally, it is not desirable
to ask for names of referees to be submitted on the application
form. To do so may make some potential candidates apprehen-
sive, even if coupled with a statement that the referees will not

be approached unless permission is granted at a later stage. It is usually better for the assessor to request the names of two or three referees towards the close of the interview, by which stage the particular points on which further evidence is needed will have been identified, and the employer can ask for referees who are in a position to supply it.

The questions put to referees need to be framed clearly and precisely. It is prudent to prepare a set of model letters so that an appropriate one can be modified, if necessary, to suit the particular circumstances before being sent to the referee. With weekly-paid operatives and clerical staff, the questions will mostly be designed to yield factual confirmation about a candidate's previous job. Especially revealing can be a final direct question such as 'Would you re-engage her for that type of work?' With more senior appointments the referee's views may be sought, additionally, on the candidate's strengths and weaknesses in relation to the job applied for, which presupposes telling the referee about the critical demands inherent in that job. In such cases, an explanatory letter to the referee arranging to telephone her or him can be a useful techniqiue. It assures the previous employer of the *bona fides* of the caller and gives an opportunity to check facts and refresh his or her memory about the candidate; and it also enables the prospective employer to take into account the manner in which the referee answers preliminary questions and to follow up, whenever necessary, with more rigorous supplementary questions.

Little reference has so far been made in this book to the practice of executive search or head-hunting, largely because much of what has already been said is equally appropriate whether the method used is executive search or advertising or by getting one's employees to introduce possible candidates. One significant variation however is in the checking out of candidates. The executive searcher, who by definition is working in a field where there are no more than, say, a maximum of 200 possible candidates, seeks to find out the reputation of each of these people by market research. This will be done by means of 'desk' search by 'using contacts'. At the desk search stage directories will be studied, as well as professional lists, professional and technical journals, national newspapers and relevant management magazines. These will all indicate who is and is not in the news, which particular companies are doing well and which are doing badly. Using a network of contacts the reputation of people is then checked. Then it is necessary to find who precisely is responsible for a company's good or bad results and who is a rising or declining star. It follows that most of this is done without the candidate's knowledge and therefore extremely discreetly. When the executive searcher has managed to narrow the list down to say 10 to 15 people they will be interviewed, so that a personal impression can be formed and the job can be 'sold' to them. Subsequently a candidate may be asked to give further referees, which may include such people as suppliers or customers or sub-contractors. But here of course the candidate is given every opportunity to contact referees in advance so that the background to the conversation may be known.

Placement and follow-up

Final assessment and placement

Summary

Towards the end of the selection process, a wealth of information about the candidate will have been gleaned from correspondence, application form, interviews and, possibly, from tests and group selection procedures. Many applicants, perhaps the majority, will have been eliminated at one or other of these hurdles. A few may have withdrawn, either because some aspect of the job holds less attraction for them than they had at first hoped or because they have accepted a different job elsewhere. The personnel manager's next important task is to reach a final assessment of each surviving candidate. This must be done in order to arrive at a positive decision or recommendation on which, if any, of them should be offered an appointment. This is done by referring again to the person specification.

In practice, constant reference will have been made to this yardstick throughout the earlier stages of the selection process. At this stage it is used to piece together all that has been learnt about each individual. Two complementary aspects are involved. Firstly, an item by item comparison of the candidate's attributes with each specific requirement of the person specification. Many interviewers find it helpful to adopt a grading scale to quantify their impressions during or immediately after the interview. A five-point scale (A, B, C, D, E) is commonly used. If finer discrimination is needed, this can be converted into a nine-point scale as follows: A, B+; B, C+; C, D+; D, E+; E. Each attribute is rated separately and is also summarized in narrative style. It is safer to use alphabetical rather than numerical gradings. With numerals it is a temptation to add up the marks awarded under each heading in order to arrive at a total assessment. This can be misleading. The separate requirements rarely, if ever, carry equal weightings. Obviously, a candidate with inadequate experience for the job should finish up with a low overall assessment even though the physical appearance may be admirable. The final assessment, therefore, cannot be simply an arithmetical average or total of the separate items. It has to be a synthesis reached after weighing all the candidates' strong and weak points. The item by item analysis should ensure that no vital point has been overlooked; but we can only employ 'the whole person', not a bundle of qualities. The second aspect therefore is a separate and final appraisal of the 'candidate as a whole' in the light of all the available evidence. This, too, can be expressed as a grade and should always be accompanied by a descriptive summary of that candidate's significant strengths and weaknesses.

A systematic method of recording assessments will facilitate the subsequent task of making comparative judgements about the respective merits of those candidates who match the person specification most closely. There is no simple formula for doing this. If one candidate stands out head and shoulders above the rest in all respects, there is no problem. More often, there may be several candidates whose overall ratings are fairly similar. The ratings themselves cannot be accepted as having absolute accuracy and consistency, since the selector's standards may have shifted slightly during the interviewing programme. The selector will be better able to differentiate between them, if each key requirement of the person specification is reconsidered and the candidates are ranked in order of merit in relation to each requirement, after having first reviewed all the relevant evidence about them. At this stage it should be possible to decide which candidate should be offered that job.

This process sounds complicated. It is; but people are complicated and it will never be a simple task to assess them fairly. In some recruitment situations, less elaborate methods have to be used, but the basic principles should still be followed. When, for example, a large number of unskilled employees has to be engaged, the personnel manager may have to concentrate on ensuring that the immediate candidate meets the person specification; and, if labour is needed urgently, a decision to engage that candidate until everybody else has been interviewed cannot be deferred, however desirable that may be in theory.

Alternatively, certain applicants may be worth considering for one of several different vacancies, in which case they must be mentally assessed against the differing demands of those jobs before a positive decision or recommendation about their engagement and placement is made. If they are equally suited to two jobs, both should be described to them and their preference taken into account.

The interviewer should ensure that a candidate does not accept a job without a clear understanding of all its conditions. The onus is on the interviewer to fulfil the second objective of the interview – to provide the candidate with an accurate picture of the job. In addition to verbal information, it is advisable wherever possible to give a more vivid picture of the job and working conditions by enabling the candidate to see it for her/himself. A visit to the department concerned is a normal routine in the final selection and placement procedure of many companies, and is usually made the occasion for meeting or having an interview with the supervisor.

A decision will have to be made about the wage or salary which is to be offered to the successful candidate. Money may not always be as decisive a factor as many people believe, but it is a profoundly important part of the contract of employment. In industry two different codes of practice often exist side by side; one for the wage earner and the other for the salary earner. The wage earner will expect to be told the rate for the job at once. It is advisable to have all the relevant information prepared in writing, giving details of basic rate, overtime rates, merit increments (if any), bonus arrangements, special allowances etc. There is no room for manoeuvre if, as is often the case, these figures are governed by an agreement with a trade union. With salary earners, things are usually different. The candidate should have gleaned from the advertisement a good idea of the salary level of the job. The employer has probably obtained a reasonably good indication of the candidate's present salary from the application form, but may be uncertain of the candidate's expectations. It is up to the employer to broach this subject and to explain the probable starting salary, the basis of salary reviews, fringe benefits and any assistance that may be offered to meet removal expenses. A precise and irrevocable figure need not necessarily be quoted during the interview; but it is desirable to establish that the approximate figure which the employer has in mind is likely to be accepted by the candidate. At the interview stage, there may still be room for negotiation and adjustment by both parties. When a firm offer has been committed to writing, there is less flexibility and neither party may be disposed to modify its position.

Contract of Employment

Not only is it statutorily obligatory, but it is basic good management practice to ensure that the new employee is fully aware of the exact nature of duties to be performed and the terms and conditions under which they should be carried out. Where this is not straightforward (particularly in managerial appointments) it is a good plan to have a further meeting before the contract is finally drawn up to discuss it in detail with the prospective employee. Many companies, aware of the impact of high taxation, are prepared to be more flexible over salary/fringe benefit than before. A candidate with a private car but high mortgage may prefer cash towards running the car rather than a company car; some may prefer a higher pension benefit than cash and so on. At this stage also the actual job description should be given to the new person and if necessary modified so as to remove any doubts. Far too often, in the author's experience, people join companies expecting one thing and discovering another on arrival. This is not deliberate (we trust!) but due to a lack of proper communications. If the proposed organization structure won't work, far better to sort it out in advance with the new employee than expect to resolve it when he or she has to sustain the full pressure of the job.

Contracts should be clear but not rigid. If the job is going to develop and change as the new employee progresses, make reference to it. A key task job description is less likely to give rise to dispute than a detailed list of duties; the latter is sure to omit some and can provide a field day for the politically motivated union official.

Besides details of hours of work, salary and benefits, job title, to whom one is responsible and where the work is located, the grievance procedure must be stated. In the past, many of these were contained in a booklet which was handed to the new employee, who was advised to read it and to sign a form to say this had been done. It is sensible to spell out the details (e.g. the company pension scheme) in a booklet but the critical points must be set out in the contract and the employer must make sure that the prospective employee understands that before joining. It is therefore usual to send a copy in advance and to run over the detail in the first morning if not before. A contract of employment, since the Contract of Employment Act (1972) and the Employment Protection (Consolidation) Act (1978), is now far more legally binding than before and both parties need to be absolutely clear as to what is agreed: for the employer, failure to do so can be very costly indeed.

What of the candidate who is eliminated? It should be borne in mind that the third objective of the interview is so to conduct it that whether the candidate is engaged or not he or she feels fair treatment has been given (see page 000). If he or she does not meet the requirements of any of the available vacancies, an effort should be made to help the candidate accept the fact. Very often it is possible to do this by pointing out those requirements of the job which are not within his or her power to meet. If this is tactfully done the candidate should be able to appreciate the wisdom of the decision. There are occasions, however, particularly where qualities of personality are involved, when it may not be possible to tell the candidate precisely why their application has been rejected. In such cases, emphasis should be placed on the useful qualities the candidate possesses, and some advice given on the type of work in which these qualities could be used.

Induction

The responsibility of the recruiter does not end when the person arrives for the first day's work. There is a period of after-care which is vitally important. Much of this can be carried out by the new employee's supervisor, but the personnel manager should ensure that it is done. He or she will have taken the first steps on receipt of the acceptance letter.

The personnel manager must try to see that the new person will be able to settle in quickly and that foreseeable problems are dealt with in advance. Peole cannot work well if they are worrying about resettling their family or finding it difficult to raise a mortgage. A leaflet giving local information and guidance on such matters can be sent to new employees before they start.

There is a limit to the amount of new information which an employee can assimilate on the first day. Everything is strange and new. Almost everyone is a stranger. The personnel manager should plan the induction programme with this in mind. Some administrative matters have to be dealt with immediately and it is sensible to have a standard checklist of these so that nothing is overlooked. The employing department can generally be made responsible for introducing the new starter to immediate colleagues and indicating the cloakroom, canteen etc. It is as well to make sure that even these obvious aspects are not left to chance. The personnel manager will usually explain welfare and personnel services as part of the induction process. The new employee can be reminded of the function of the personnel department and encouraged to raise any settling-in problems so that these can be nipped in the bud before they develop into serious difficulties. It is advisable to visit each new starter at the place of work during the first few days. This need not take more than a couple of minutes but is the best way of making sure that all is going well.

New employees want to prove their worth as soon as possible after their arrival. The more quickly they are helped to find their feet, the better will be their impression of the company they have joined.

Follow-up of results

At this point the most crucial stage of selection work has not even started yet. Nor could it have been.

The whole purpose of recruiting is to find people who will prove to be well matched to the jobs for which they are engaged. It is certainly not to produce a succession of new starters. Knowledge of results is essential. The personnel manager cannot know whether the new employee's performance is satisfactory unless there is a systematic feedback of information about the employee's progress. This concept of feedback is most important, if high standards of attainment are to be reached in any field of human endeavour. The efficacy of selection work must be judged by its actual results.

Neglect of follow-up can have serious consequences. A poor selector may remain undetected for a long time and a considerable amount of money may be wasted through unnecessarily high labour turnover, or in training the wrong people. Furthermore, however sound the selection methods may be, some mistakes will occur, and when they do they should be remedied as soon as possible.

Like the preceding stages of the selection procedure, the follow-up must be systematic. An initial check should be made not later than one month after the date of engagement. The employee's supervisor or head of department should be asked to report the performance of the newcomer, basing that assessment on the requirements of the original job/person specifications. If the report indicates that the employee is not settling in well, the personnel manager must ascertain the reason. After discussion with the supervisor, it may be decided to provide additional training, to offer the employee a transfer to a different job or to await the outcome of a further follow-up. Whether the report shows a satisfactory performance or not, the employee should be told frankly at a private interview with the supervisor how he or she is progressing.

A single follow-up can seldom provide a sound basis for judging whether an employee has been suitably placed. A careful report after the first month may be adequate in the case of certain simple routine jobs. But when the work is complex, as in the case of executive appointments, or where there is a prolonged period of training, as in apprenticeships, a series of reports at regular intervals will be necessary. In companies that already operate a system of periodic assessment of all employees – whether this be done primarily for salary reviews, merit awards, training, promotion potential etc – information of value to the selector can be an additional by-product. If no such reporting system exists, the selector must institute follow-up procedures.

Whenever the results of a follow-up are at a variance with the selector's original assessment of an employee, the selection records should be carefully scrutinized for possible clues. This is made easier if comparable rating scales are used to record both the interview and the follow-up. If evidence is found that the selector repeatedly misjudges a particular attribute, he or she will know that extra attention must be paid to the methods of evaluating that attribute in future. Correlation of selection predictions with the candidate's subsequent performance is a necessary step towards the development of better selection procedures and greater skill in matching candidates and jobs.

Recruitment administration

Efficient recruitment includes a good deal of longer term preparation. The recruiter's task is facilitated if potential candidates can be predisposed to think they would like to work for the company. They are more likely to apply if they already regard the firm as a good employer. A good reputation has to be earned over the years. It can be consolidated or undermined by the way in which recruitment is conducted. Therefore the personnel manager must be sensitive to the climate of public opinion and must be concerned with the company's reputation or image as an employer. There is much that the personnel manager can contribute in that respect.

Over a period, attitudes can be influenced by the content and style of recruitment advertisements, particularly by those appearing in local newspapers which are used frequently. The advertisements can be regarded as an information channel through which to stimulate interest in developments taking place within the company and to convey something of its character, as well as serving the immediate purpose of publicizing specific jobs.

The planned release to the local newspapers of advance information on newsworthy developments is also a practical method of paving the way for recruitment, especially if it heralds a major expansion; and personnel managers should therefore keep in close touch with their editorial staffs. In fact, they should make it their business to know personally all those who are regularly concerned, directly or indirectly, with recruitment in that locality. This will include, for example, the manager of the local branch of the Department of Employment, youth employment officers, head teachers and careers teachers etc. Links with technical colleges may lead to requests for the company's products or processes to be included in displays or demonstrations. Representation on regional planning committees, participation in local exhibitions and occasional factory visits can all have some bearing on the long term task of building and sustaining the company's reputation. With forethought, much can be done that will facilitate the future engagement of the right calibre of employees at the time when they are needed.

Recruitment policy and procedures can and should be summarized in the form of a reference manual, the appropriate sections of which are held by each member of the staff who has a part to play. Whilst emphasizing the personal and confidential nature of recruitment, it should contain guidance on practical aspects such as the role of the recruiter *vis-à-vis* the line manager; standing instructions to gate-keepers, receptionists and telephonists; rules governing the reimbursement of travel expenses; personnel records to be completed; the use of model letters or printed reply slips; maximum time lapse permitted in dealing with applications; procedures for taking up references etc. It is neither possible nor desirable to legislate for every contingency, and room must always be left for the application of common sense. The manual must be reviewed periodically to ensure that administrative practices remain consistent with the basic policy intentions.

Applicants' early impressions of a company are influenced by the stationery and recruitment forms adopted. These should be well designed with simple and clear headings. Model letters to cover frequently recurring situations can be used to save both dictation and transcription time. They should be modified, as appropriate, to meet individual circumstances; and care must be taken lest specific questions asked by the candidate are ignored.

Printed acknowledgement slips and standard letters can help to ensure that each applicant receives a prompt reply and can save a good deal of staff time when confronted with a large number of applications. Carefully worded, they can be acceptable in some situations but, since they lack the personal touch, procedures regulating their use should be drawn up carefully.

Courteous reception depends on having suitably trained people as gate-keepers and receptionists. Signposts pointing the way to the personnel office should be installed on large sites. The waiting room need not be elaborately furnished, but it should be well lit and kept tidy. A mirror should be provided and there should be access to nearby lavatories. A table with writing materials will be needed for the completion of application forms and there must be a sufficient number of upright and reclining chairs. Up to date reading matter should be at hand and this may include literature about the company and its products as well as newspapers and periodicals. One member of the staff should be made explicitly responsible for seeing that the waiting room is maintained in good order at all times. Old magazines and burned out electric light bulbs present a poor impression of the company's standard of efficiency. Attention to detail and unfailing courtesy are the marks of the good administrator and imply that the company is genuinely interested in people.

Summary of typical procedures

To sum up, a typical recruitment programme might comprise at least a score of separate actions carried out in the sequence below. Each one is important. Mistakes often arise because insufficient attention is devoted to the earlier steps in the recruitment process.

1 Receive employee requisition (on standard form) from department manager.
2 Search files for the relevant job/person specification or for a similar one.
3 Discuss vacancy with supervisor, ensure that replacement is absolutely necessary, and arrange to interview present incumbent to explore reasons for leaving.
4 Review and modify job/person specification in the light of changes which may have taken place and agree these with supervisor and department manager.
5 Consider feasibility of internal promotion or transfer; failing which, determine the most probable sources of candidates and the most economical method of attracting them. Check whether any enquiries have been received from suitably qualified people in recent months.
6 Inform Department of Employment, employment agencies and/or prepare draft advertisement and select the most appropriate advertising media.
7 On receipt of applications, classify provisionally into (a) most likely, (b) possible, (c) unsuitable. Write or telephone promptly to (a) arranging interview if time is short and ask for completed application form to be returned with confirmation;

send 'model' letter to (b) with application form; eliminate (c) unless suitable for alternative vacancy.

8 Acknowledge receipt of application forms and scrutinize for additional candidates who merit interview.

9 Conduct preliminary interviews, and use other assessment techniques as appropriate. (Note any candidate's travelling expenses.)

10 Compile shortlist, agree arrangements for final selection procedure with department manager.

11 Invite shortlisted candidates and arrange overnight accommodation if needed. Write to other interviewed candidates advising them that they have been unsuccessful.

12 Send copy of timetable to all staff affected, reserve interviewing rooms, order coffee, inform receptionist etc.

13 Conduct final assessment programme.

14 Prepare letter of appointment for successful candidate and agree arrangements for verifying qualifications, taking up references and attending medical examination with the candidate.

15 On confirmation of acceptance, write to unsuccessful candidates (and to any others who have not been turned down). In appropriate cases advise them that they will be considered for any suitable future vacancies which may arise.

16 Write 'starting instructions' letter to successful candidate.

17 Make out personnel records for new employee and inform department, accounts offices etc of proposed starting date.

18 See that induction procedures are carried out.

19 Preliminary follow-up within one month to resolve any settling-in difficulties.

20 Subsequent follow-up and comparison of progress report with original selection assessment and predictions.

Final note

The follow-up reports will produce some disappointments. No selector can expect to be proved right in every assessment ever made. They can be expected, however, to search relentlessly for ways of avoiding those mistakes and cannot be forgiven if they go on repeating them; the costs are too great. Recruitment and selection work must be carried out competently and conscientiously or a trail of industrial inefficiency and unhappiness may follow it its wake. Those engaged in this work, whether regularly or occasionally, must always be mindful of the personal responsibilities they carry. People make companies. And the selector chooses those people. But recruitment and selection work is not carried out in a vacuum and its results cannot be judged as though it were. It forms only one part of personnel management, albeit a most important part; and as with any other branch of personnel work its full benefits will accrue only where the company's personnel policy as a whole is sound.

Selected Bibliography

Recruitment

ADVISORY, CONCILIATION AND ARBITRATION SERVICE. *Recruitment and selection.* London, ACAS, 1983. (Advisory booklet 6)

APEX TRUST. *Releasing the potential: a guide to good practice for the employment of people with criminal records.* London, Next Step Training, 1990

BAIRD Robert B. *The executive grapevine 1990.* London, Executive Grapevine, 1990

COLLINSON David *and* KNIGHTS David. *Managing to discriminate.* London, Routledge, 1990

CONNOR Helen, BUCHAN James *and* PEARSON Richard. *The changing IT skills scene: the IT manpower monitor 1989.* Falmer, IMS, 1989

COURTIS John. *Recruiting for profit.* London, Institute of Personnel Management, 1989

ELECTRONICS INDUSTRY SECTOR GROUP/IMS. *Switching on skills: new approaches to skill shortages in UK electronics and IT.* London, NEDO, 1989

FINNIGAN John. *The right people in the right jobs.* 2nd ed. Aldershot, Gower, 1983

HERRIOT Peter. *Recruitment in the 90s.* London, Institute of Personnel Management, 1989

HIGHTON Linda *and* ZAHNO Kamila. *More choice, better workforce: solving recruitment problems in the 90s.* London, Southwark Council, 1990

HUBBARD G. 'The recruitment jungle'. *Management Today*. September 1984. pp 84–86, 88

INSTITUTE OF PERSONNEL MANAGEMENT. *The IPM recruitment code.* 3rd ed. London, IPM, 1983

INSTITUTE OF PERSONNEL MANAGEMENT. *The IPM equal opportunities code.* London, IPM, 1990

INSTITUTE OF PERSONNEL MANAGEMENT *and* BRITISH INSTITUTE OF MANAGEMENT. *Selecting managers: how British industry recruits.* London, IPM/BIM, 1980. (IPM information report 34; BIM management survey report 49).

'In the name of the law'. Employment law supplement to *Personnel Today*, 6–19 February 1990

JACKSON Matthew. *Recruiting, interviewing and selecting: a manual for line managers.* London, McGraw-Hill, 1972

LEIGHTON Patricia, *ed. The Daily Telegraph recruitment handbook.* 3rd ed. London, Kogan Page, 1990

MANGUM S L. 'Recruitment and job search: the recruitment tactics of employers'. *Personnel Administrator.* Vol 27, No 6, June 1982. pp 96, 99–102, 104

NEWELL David. *Understanding recruitment law.* London, Waterlow, 1984

PEARSON Richard *and* WALSH Kenneth. *How to analyse your local labour market.* Aldershot, Gower, 1983. (Institute of Manpower Studies series 2)

P E INTERNATIONAL. *Personnel policies in Europe.* Egham, P E International, 1990

PLUMBLEY Philip *and* WILLIAMS Roger. *The person for the job: the complete guide to successful recruitment and selection.* 2nd ed. London, Kogan Page, 1981

PRICE WATERHOUSE CRANFIELD. *Project on international strategic human resource management: 1990 report.* London, Price Waterhouse in association with Cranfield School of Management, 1990

'Recruiting with the rules'. *Employment Digest.* No 149, January 9, 1984. pp 1, 8

Recruitment and selection. Bicester, CCH Editions, 1985. (Personnel management in practice 1)

SMITH Edwin. *Skills needs in Britain 1990.* London, IFF Research in association with the Training Agency, 1990

STOOPS R. 'Managing recruitment costs'. *Personnel Journal.* Vol 62, No 8, August 1983. pp 612, 615

SUTER Erich. *The employment law checklist.* 4th ed. London, Institute of Personnel Management, 1990

UNGERSON Bernard, *ed. Recruitment handbook.* 3rd ed. Aldershot, Gower, 1983

WALSH Kenneth *and* PEARSON Richard. *UK labour market guide.* Aldershot, Gower, 1984. (Institute of Manpower Studies series 5)

WANOUS John P. *Organizational entry: recruitment, selection and socialization of newcomers.* Reading, Mass, Addison-Wesley, 1980

Job Analysis

ASH R A *and* LEVINE E L. 'A framework for evaluating job analysis methods'. *Personnel.* Vol 57, No 6, November/December 1980. pp 53–59

BEMIS Stephen E, BELENKY Ann Holt *and* SODER Dee Ann. *Job analysis: an effective management tool.* Washington, D.C., Bureau of National Affairs, 1983

BOYDELL T H. *A guide to job analysis*. London, British Association for Commercial and Industrial Education, 1973

MCCORMICK Ernest J. *Job analysis: methods and applications*. New York, American Management Association, 1979

MARKOWITZ J. 'Four methods of job analysis'. *Training and Development Journal*. Vol 35, No 9, September 1981. pp 112–15, 117–18

PEARN Michael *and* KANDOLA Rajvinder. *Job analysis*. London, Institute of Personnel Management, 1988

YOUNGMAN Michael Brendon *and others. Analysing jobs*. Farnborough, Gower/Teakfield, 1978

Job Descriptions

AUSTIN D L. 'A new approach to position descriptions'. *Personnel Journal*. Vol 56, No 7, July 1977. pp 354–55, 363, 365–66

JONES M A. 'Job descriptions made easy'. *Personnel Journal*. Vol 63, No 5, May 1984, pp 31–4

KLINGER D E. 'When the traditional job description is not enough'. *Personnel Journal*. Vol 58, No 4, April 1979. pp 243–48

UNGERSON Bernard. *How to write a job description*. London, Institute of Personnel Management, 1983

WEBB Sue. 'Preparing and using job descriptions'. *Employment Bulletin*. Vol 1, No 8, November 1984. pp 58–61

Recruitment Methods

CHEMICAL INDUSTRIES ASSOCIATION. *Graduate recruitment survey*. London, Chemical Industries Association, 1989

CLARK T A R. *The executive and search industry: an analysis of an emergent industry.* Coventry, Leicester Polytechnic, 1988

COWTON C J. 'To advertise or to use a recruitment bureau'. *Management Decision.* Vol 21, No 6, 1983. pp 31–8

FRANKS Alan. 'Golden hello or gilt handcuffs?' *Times,* 30 October 1989

'Headhunting: how the executive search game is played'. *Personnel Executive.* Vol 1, No 3, September 1981. pp 28–31

HERRIOT Peter. *Assessment and selection in organizations: methods and practice for recruitment and appraisal.* Chichester, Wiley, 1989

HOARE D. 'Helping the headhunter get his man'. *Management Today.* November 1984. pp 41, 45, 48

LOCAL AUTHORITIES CONDITIONS OF SERVICE ADVISORY BOARD. *Recruiting and retaining computer staff in local authorities.* London, LACSAB, 1990

LUBLINER M J. 'Developing recruitment literature that pays off'. *Personnel Administrator.* Vol 26, No 2, February 1981. pp 51–4, 95

MSL ADVERTISING. *Looking ahead – recruitment in the 1990s.* London, MSL Advertising, 1989

RAY Maurice. *Recruitment advertising: a means of communication.* London, Institute of Personnel Management, 1980

RUGMAN N. 'Rooting out recruits: headhunting versus standard search'. *Personnel Management.* Vol 11, No 6, June 1979. pp 42–4

SCHOFIELD Philip. 'Getting the best from recruitment agencies'. *Personnel Management.* Vol 13, No 8, August 1981. pp 40–3

STORER Gary. *Recruiting young people in the 1990s.* London, Kogan Page, 1990

UNIVERSITY OF SUSSEX. *The 1989 milkround – figures and trends.* Falmer, Careers Advisory Service, 1989

Selection

GILL Deirdre. 'How British industry selects its managers'. *Personnel Management.* Vol 12, No 9, September 1980. pp 49–52

HOLDSWORTH R. 'Selection tips for small firm managers'. *Personnel Management.* Vol 7, No 3, March 1975. pp 31–3

INSTITUTE OF PERSONNEL MANAGEMENT. 'Executive search', Factsheet No. 31, inserted in *Personnel Management*, July 1990

INSTITUTE OF PERSONNEL MANAGEMENT. JOINT STANDING COMMITTEE ON DISCRIMINATION. *Towards fairer selection: a code for non-discrimination.* London, IPM, 1978

JEFFERY R. 'Taking the guesswork out of selection'. *Personnel Management.* Vol 9, No 10, October 1977. pp 40–2

LEWIS C. 'What's new in . . . selection'. *Personnel Management.* Vol 16, No 1, January 1984. pp 14–6

MACKENZIE-DAVEY D *and* HARRIS Marjorie, *eds. Judging people: a guide to orthodox and unorthodox methods of assessment.* London, McGraw-Hill, 1983

MEYER John L *and* DONAHO Melvin W. *Get the right person for the job: managing interviews and selecting employees.* Englewood Cliffs, N.J., Prentice Hall, 1979

OWENS D *and* HARROWVEN L. 'How to cope with a flood of job applications'. *Perspective.* January 1982. pp 4–5

SHACKLETON Viv. *How to pick people for jobs.* London, Fontana, 1989

Application Forms

DYER Barbara. *Personnel systems and records.* 3rd ed. London, Gower, 1979

KEENAN T. 'Where application forms mislead'. *Personnel Management.* Vol 15, No 2, February 1983. pp 40–3

PENDLEBURY C. 'Application form design'. *Industrial and Commercial Training.* Vol 2, No 11, November 1970. pp 527–29

Selection Interviewing

ANSTEY Edgar. *An introduction to selection interviewing.* London, HMSO, 1977

ARVEY R D *and* CAMPION J E. 'The employment interview: a summary and review of recent research'. *Personnel Psychology.* Vol 35, No 2, Summer 1982. pp 281–322

AUSTIN D L. 'Interviewing candidates for managerial positions'. *Personnel Journal.* Vol 62, No 3, March 1983. pp 192–94

BAYNE R. 'Can selection interviewing be improved?' *Journal of Occupational Psychology.* Vol 50, No 3, 1977. pp 161–67

BOLTON G M. *Interviewing for selection decisions.* Windsor, NFER-Nelson, 1983

Croner's guide to interviews. New Malden, Croner Publications, 1985

FRASER John Munro. *Employment interviewing.* 5th ed. London, Macdonald and Evans 1978

GOODALE James G. *The fine art of interviewing.* Englewood Cliffs, N.J., Prentice Hall, 1982

GOODWORTH Clive T. *Effective interviewing for employment selection.* London, Business Books, 1979

GREEN J. 'Structured sequence interviewing'. *Personnel Executive.* Vol 2, No 10, April 1983. pp 26–7, 29

GRUMMIT Janis. *A guide to interviewing skills.* London, Industrial Society, 1980

HACKETT Penny. *Interview skills training: practice packs for trainers.* 2nd ed. London, Institute of Personnel Management, 1991

HIGHAM M. *The ABC of interviewing.* London, Institute of Personnel Management, 1979

KAHN Robert L *and* CANNELL Charles F. *The dynamics of interviewing.* New York, Wiley, 1957

LOCK Harold F. *Interviewing for selection.* 4th ed. London, National Institute for Industrial Psychology, 1972. (NIIP paper 3)

MACKAY Ian. *A guide to asking questions.* London, British Association for Commercial and Industrial Education, 1980

MACKENZIE-DAVEY D *and* MCDONNELL P. *How to interview.* London, British Institute of Management, 1975

PALMER Robin. 'A sharper focus for the panel interview'. *Personnel Management.* Vol 15, No 5, May 1983, pp 34–7

PURSELL E D, *and others.* 'Structured interviewing: avoiding selection problems'. *Personnel Journal.* Vol 59, No 11, November 1980. pp 907–12

RODGER Alec. *The seven-point plan.* 3rd ed. London, National Institute of Industrial Psychology, 1970. (NIIP paper 1)

SCHWEITZER N J *and* DEELY J. 'Interviewing the disabled job applicant'. *Personnel Journal.* Vol 61, No 3, March 1982. pp 205–09

THARP C G. 'A manager's guide to selection interviewing'. *Personnel Journal*. Vol 62, No 8, August 1983. pp 636–39

WHITTAKER Peter. *Selection interviewing*. Rev. ed. London, Industrial Society, 1977. (Notes for managers 24)

Group Selection

ANSTEY E. 'The Civil Service administrative class: a follow-up of post-war entrants'. *Occupational Psychology*. Vol 45, No 1, 1971. pp 27–43

ANSTEY E. 'The Civil Service administrative class: extended interview selection procedure'. *Occupational Psychology*. Vol 45, No 3/4, 1971. pp 199–208

ANSTEY E. 'A 30 year follow-up of the CSSB procedure, with lessons for the future'. *Journal of Occupational Psychology*. Vol 50, No 3, 1977. pp 149–59

BRUSH D H *and* SCHOENFELDT L F. 'Identifying managerial potential: an alternative to assessment centres'. *Personnel*. Vol 57, No 3, May/June 1980. pp 68–76

BYHAM William C. 'Assessing employees without resorting to a centre'. *Personnel Management*. October 1984, pp 56–7

CIVIL SERVICE COMMISSION. *Report of the committee on the selection procedure for the recruitment of administration trainees*. London, Civil Service Commission, 1979

COHEN S L. 'Pre-packaged *vs* tailor made: the assessment centre debate'. *Personnel Journal*. Vol 59, No 12, December 1980. pp 989–91

FIELDS H. 'The group interview test: its strength'. *Public Personnel Review*. July 1950. pp 139–46

FINKLE Robert B. 'Managerial assessment centres'. pp 861–88 *in* DUNNETTE Marvin D, *ed*. *Handbook of industrial and organizational psychology*. Chicago, Rand McNally, 1976

FRASER J M. 'An experiment with group methods in the selection of trainees for senior management positions'. *Occupational Psychology*. Vol 20, No 2, April 1946. pp 63–7

HIGHAM M H. 'Some recent work with group selection techniques'. *Occupational Psychology*. Vol 26, No 3, July 1952. pp 169–75

KEIL E C. *Assessment centers: a guide for human resource management*. Reading, Mass., Addison-Wesley, 1981

KNOWLES M C. 'Group assessment in staff selection'. *Personnel Practice Bulletin*. June 1983. pp 6–16

MACRAE Angus. *Group selection procedures*. 2nd ed. Windsor, NFER Publishing, 1970 (NIIP paper 5)

The Method II system of selection (for the administrative class of the Home Civil Service): report of the Committee of Inquiry, 1969. London, HMSO, 1969

MORRIS Ben S. 'Officer selection in the British Army, 1942–1945'. *Occupational Psychology*. Vol 23, No 4, October 1949. pp 219–34 *and* Vol 24, No 1, January 1950. pp 54–61

MOSES Joseph L *and* BYHAM William C, *eds*. *Applying the assessment centre method*. New York, Pergamon, 1977

NATIONAL AUDIT OFFICE. *Clerical recruitment in the Civil Service: report by the Comptroller and Auditor General*. London, HMSO, 1990

STEWART Andrew. *A way to find new managers*. Falmer, Institute of Manpower Studies, 1981

STEWART Andrew *and* STEWART Valerie. *Tomorrow's managers today: the identification and development of management potential.* 2nd ed. London, Institute of Personnel Management, 1981.

THORNTON George C *and* BYHAM William C. *Assessment centres and managerial performance.* London, Academic Press, 1982.

UNGERSON Bernard. 'Assessment centres: a review of research findings'. *Personnel Review.* Vol 3, No 3, Summer 1974. pp 4–13

VERNON Philip E. 'The validation of Civil Service Selection Board procedures'. *Occupational Psychology.* Vol 24, No 2, April 1950. pp 75–95

VERNON Philip E *and* PARRY John B. *Personnel selection in the British Forces.* London, University of London Press, 1949

Testing

AIKEN Lewis R. *Psychological testing and assessment.* 4th ed. Boston, Mass., Allyn and Bacon, 1982

ANASTASI Anne. *Psychological testing.* 5th ed. London, Collier-Macmillan, 1982

BARTRAM D *and* BAYLISS R. 'Automated testing: past, present and future'. *Journal of Occupational Psychology.* Vol 57, No 3, 1984. pp 221–31

BOLTON G M. *Testing in selection decisions.* Windsor, NFER-Nelson, 1983

CRONBACH Lee Joseph. *Essentials of psychological testing.* 4th ed. New York, Harper and Row, 1984

DULEWICZ V. 'Uses and abuses of selection tests'. *Personnel Management.* Vol 16, No 1, January 1984. pp 46–7

GUION Robert M. 'Recruiting, selection and job placement'. pp 777–828 in DUNNETTE Marvin D, ed. *Handbook of industrial and organizational psychology*. Chicago, Rand McNally, 1976

HOLDSWORTH R F. *Personnel selection testing: a guide for managers*. London, British Institute of Management, 1972

INSTITUTE OF PERSONNEL MANAGEMENT. 'Psychological Testing'. Factsheet No 24, inserted in *Personnel Management*, December 1989

JESSUP Gilbert *and* JESSUP Helen. *Selection and assessment at work*. London, Methuen, 1975.

PEARN Michael A. *The fair use of selection tests*. Windsor, NFER Publishing, n.d.

SNEATH Frank, THAKUR Manub *and* MEDJUCK Bruce. *Testing people at work*. London, Institute of Personnel Management, 1976. (Information report 24)

STEWART Andrew M *and* STEWART Valerie. *Tests in personnel selection: the use of psychological tests in industry*. Uxbridge, Brunel University, Institute of Organizational and Social Studies, n.d.

TOPLIS John, DULEWICZ Vic *and* FLETCHER Clive. *Psychological Testing*. 2nd ed. London, Institute of Personnel Management, 1991.

TYLER Leona E *and* WALSH W Bruce. *Tests and measurements*. 3rd ed. Englewood Cliffs, N.J., Prentice-Hall, 1979

'Using selection tests in recruitment and promotion'. *Industrial Relations Review and Report*. No 177, June 1978. pp 2–9

VERNON Philip E. *Intelligence testing 1928–1978: what next?* Edinburgh, Scottish Council for Research in Education, 1979

References

LEVINE Edward L *and* RUDOLPH Stephen M. *Reference checking for personnel selection: the state of the art.* Ohio, American Society for Personnel Administration, 1978

'References: a safety net, but they're no substitute for good judgement'. *Perspective.* August 1983, p 5

Induction

ADVISORY, CONCILIATION AND ARBITRATION SERVICE. *Induction of new employees.* London, ACAS, 1982. (Advisory booklet 7)

'Company induction programmes'. *Industrial Relations Review and Report.* No 173, April 1978. pp 2–5

FOWLER Alan E. *A good start: successful employee induction.* London, Institute of Personnel Management, 1990

INDUSTRIAL SOCIETY. *Induction.* London, Industrial Society, 1973. (Notes for managers 21)

MARKS Winifred R. *Induction: acclimatizing people to work.* Rev. ed. London, Institute of Personnel Management, 1974

ST JOHN W D. 'The complete employee orientation program'. *Personnel Journal.* Vol 58, No 5, May 1980, pp 373–78

SHEA Gordon F. *The new employee: developing a productive human resource.* Reading, Mass., Addison-Wesley, 1981

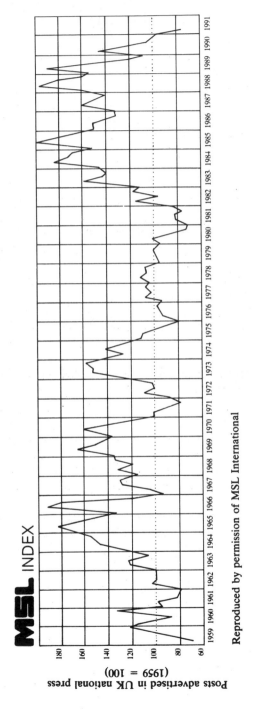

Reproduced by permission of MSL International

Figure 1   The rate of demand for Managers and Executives since 1959

UNITED KINGDOM ADVERTISED DEMAND FOR MANAGERS AND KEY SPECIALIST STAFF
(12 months to March 31)

Type of work	1990–91		1989–90		1988–89		1987–88		1986–87	
	Posts advertised	Change from 89–90 %	Posts advertised	Change from 88–89 %	Posts advertised	Change from 87–88 %	Posts advertised	Change from 86–87 %	Posts advertised	Change from 85–86 %
Research and Development	2,849	−23.8	3,738	−14.1	4,353	+24.0	3,510	+ 3.9	3,378	−42.0
Sales and marketing	2,630	−24.4	3,480	−32.6	5,164	−19.0	6,373	+ 4.1	6,124	− 5.0
Production	4,276	−26.6	5,823	−20.3	7,309	+17.1	6,242	+29.9	4,807	−23.8
Accounting	4,462	−32.3	6,588	−13.3	7,602	− 2.5	7,795	+15.8	6,732	+ 5.2
Computing	1,870	−37.6	2,999	−38.5	4,878	+31.5	3,710	+ 0.7	3,686	− 7.8
General management	1,213	− 8.3	1,323	−15.2	1,561	− 5.9	1,659	+19.8	1,385	+ 6.0
Personnel	623	−41.4	1,063	− 4.7	1,115	− 0.2	1,117	+11.1	1,005	+15.5
Others	5,739	−18.5	7,044	−11.0	7,912	+14.1	6,936	+20.9	5,735	− 6.9
Total	**23,662**	**−26.2**	**32,058**	**−19.6**	**39,894**	**+ 6.8**	**37,342**	**+13.7**	**32,852**	**−12.0**
April-June	7,641	−16.7	9,176	−13.4	10,593	+23.2	8,597	+ 5.2	8,172	−21.5
July-Sept	6,131	−22.0	7,858	−15.8	9,338	+12.9	8,274	+ 8.0	7,664	−19.4
Oct-Dec	5,318	−19.8	6,627	−26.8	9,048	− 2.2	9,248	+17.8	7,850	− 8.7
Jan-March	4,572	−45.6	8,397	−23.1	10,915	− 2.7	11,223	+22.4	9,166	+ 4.1

Reproduced by permission of MSL International

The demand for executives has been shown over the years to follow a cyclical pattern as industry and services gear up or decline in line with – and often in advance of – movements in the economy. Recovery is usually led by R & D followed by Production, then Sales and Marketing, then the Service and Control functions; decline in R & D often presages a decline in other functions in the order reversed. These changes in functional demand are partly responsible for the apparent shortages of executives at specific times, i.e. shortage is a function of demand rather than an absolute in many cases. It may also reflect a sudden change in the nature of the demand; e.g. in the mid-70's there was a sudden demand for US-trained management accountants; in the mid-80's for academically trained IT staff etc.

Table 1 (opposite) Sectoral trends in the demand for executives